THE LIBRARY OF HOLOCAUST TESTIMONIES

From Berlin to England and Back
Experiences of a Jewish Berliner

The Library of Holocaust Testimonies

Editors: Antony Polonsky, SirMartin Gilbert CBE,
Aubrey Newman, Raphael F. Scharf, Ben Helfgott MBE

Under the auspices of the Yad Vashem Committee of the Board of
Deputies of British Jews and the Centre for Holocaust Studies,
University of Leicester

My Lost World by Sara Rosen
From Dachau to Dunkirk by Fred Pelican
Breathe Deeply, My Son by Henry Wermuth
My Private War by Jacob Gerstenfeld-Maltiel
A Cat Called Adolf by Trude Levi
An End to Childhood by Miriam Akavia
A Child Alone by Martha Blend
The Children Accuse by Maria Hochberg-Marianska and Noe Gruss
I Light a Candle by Gena Turgel
My Heart in a Suitcase by Anne L. Fox
Memoirs from Occupied Warsaw, 1942–1945
by Helena Szereszewska
Have You Seen My Little Sister? by Janina Fischler-Martinho
Surviving the Nazis, Exile and Siberia by Edith Sekules
Out of the Ghetto by Jack Klajman with Ed Klajman
From Thessaloniki to Auschwitz and Back
by Erika Myriam Kounio Amariglio
Translated by Theresa Sundt
I Was No. 20832 at Auschwitz by Eva Tichauer
Translated by Colette Lévy and Nicki Rensten
My Child is Back! by Ursula Pawel
Wartime Experiences in Lithuania by Rivka Lozansky Bogomolnaya
Translated by Miriam Beckerman
Who Are You, Mr Grymek? by Natan Gross
Translated by William Brand
A Life Sentence of Memories by Issy Hahn, Foreword by
Theo Richmond
An Englishman in Auschwitz by Leon Greenman
For Love of Life by Leah Iglinsky-Goodman
No Place to Run: A True Story by Tim Shortridge and
Michael D. Frounfelter
A Little House on Mount Carmel by Alexandre Blumstein
From Germany to England Via the Kindertransports by Peter Prager
By a Twist of History: The Three Lives of a Polish Jew by Mietek Sieradzki
The Jews of Poznań by Zbigniew Pakula
Lessons in Fear by Henryk Vogler

From Berlin to England and Back
Experiences of a Jewish Berliner

PETER PRAGER

VALLENTINE MITCHELL
LONDON • PORTLAND, OR

First Published in 2002 in Great Britain by
VALLENTINE MITCHELL
Crown House, 47 Chase Side
Southgate, London N14 5BP

and in the United States of America by
VALLENTINE MITCHELL
c/o ISBS, 5824 N. E. Hassalo Street
Portland, Oregon, 97213-3644

Website: http://www.vmbooks.com

British Library Cataloguing in Publication Data

Prager, Peter
    From Berlin to England and back: experiences of a Jewish Berliner. –
    (The library of Holocaust testimonies)
    1. Prager, Peter 2. Jewish teachers – Germany – Berlin – Biography 3.
    Jewish teachers – Great Britain – Biography 4. World War, 1939–1945
    – Evacuation of civilians – Germany
    I.Title
    940.5'318'

ISBN 0-85303-420-6 (paper)
ISSN 1363-3759

Library of Congress Cataloging-in-Publication Data

Prager, Peter, 1923–
    From Berlin to England and back: experiences of a Jewish
    Berliner/Peter Prager.
        p.cm. – (Library of Holocaust testimonies)
    ISBN 0-85303-420-6 (pbk.)
    1. Prager, Peter, 1923 – 2. Jews – Germany – Biography. 3. Holocaust,
    Jewish (1939–1945) – Germany – Berlin. 4. Refugees, Jewish – England
    – Biography. 5. Berlin (Germany) – Biography. I. Title II. Series.

DS135.G5 P727 2002
943'.155004924'0092–dc21
[B]
                                                            2002075368

Typeset in 11 on 13pt Palatino by FiSH Books.
Printed in Great Britain by MPG Books Ltd, Victoria Square, Bodmin,
Cornwall

To my wife, Sylvia,
who tutored and edited throughout

Contents

Contents

List of Illustrations

The Library of Holocaust Testimonies

It is greatly to the credit of Frank Cass that this series of survivors' testimonies is being published in Britain. The need for such a series has been long apparent, where many survivors made their homes.

Since the end of the war in 1945 the terrible events of the Nazi destruction of European Jewry have cast a pall over our time. Six million Jews were murdered within a short period; the few survivors have had to carry in their memories whatever remains of the knowledge of Jewish life in more than a dozen countries, in several thousand towns, in tens of thousands of villages, and in innumerable families. The precious gift of recollection has been the sole memorial for millions of people whose lives were suddenly and brutally cut off.

For many years, individual survivors have published their testimonies. But many more have been reluctant to do so, often because they could not believe that they would find a publisher for their efforts.

In my own work over the past two decades I have been approached by many survivors who had set down their memories in writing, but who did not know how to have them published. I also realized, as I read many dozens of such accounts, how important each account was, in its own way, in recounting aspects of the story that had not been told before, and adding to our understanding of the wide range of human suffering, struggle and aspiration.

With so many people and so many places involved, including many hundreds of camps, it was inevitable that the historians and students of the Holocaust should find it difficult at times to grasp the scale and range of events. The publication of memoirs is therefore an indispensable part of the extension of knowledge, and of public awareness of the crimes that had been committed against a whole people.

Sir Martin Gilbert
Merton College, Oxford

Chronology

1812   Jews living in Prussia receive Prussian citizenship.

1820   Great-grandfather Prager moves from Silesia to Berlin.

1821   The founding of Kofferfabrik Prager.

1842   Grandfather Leopold Prager is born.

1849   Grandfather Blumenthal is born in Bromberg, Poznan.

1876   Father Paul Prager is born.

1897   Kofferfabrik L. Prager is appointed supplier to the Kaiser and King of Prussia.

1898   Mother, Nanny Blumenthal, is born in Bromberg.

1908   Mother marries her first husband.

1910   Hans, my brother, is born.

1915   Mother's first husband dies in a home for morphine addicts.

1920   Mother marries father.

1923   The author, Peter, is born.

1930   Mother divorces father and marries Onkel Franz, a Christian.

1936   Kofferfabrik L. Prager is taken over by the Nazis.

1938   On 31 December Peter arrives in England in a Kindertransport.

1939   Father arrives in England.

1944   Onkel Franz is sent to a forced labour camp to compel him to divorce Mother; he is tortured, but refuses, thus enabling Mother to survive.

1946   Father dies.

1947   Onkel Franz dies; Mother joins me and Hans in England.

1949   Mother dies.

1 Berlin

On 11 March 1920 Vati as usual boarded the bus reading the *Berliner Tageblatt*. The bus rolled along the Kurfürstendamm towards the centre of town. At the Siegesallee, in sight of the Brandenburg Gate, it came to an abrupt halt. Armed soldiers blocked the way. The soldiers displayed the flag of the Kaiser – black, white and red. How could this be? The Kaiser had abdicated 18 months earlier and the new flag of the republic was black, red and gold. While Vati was trying to work this out, a low-flying plane roared overhead. They were showered with leaflets, and all the passengers scrambled out of the bus to read them.

Proclamation to the German people!
The Reich and the Nation are in danger! The government is not capable of warding off bolshevism. The Reich government has ceased to exist. Dr von Kapp has taken over the post of Reich Chancellor and Prime Minister of Prussia. The new military commander and Minister of Defence is General von Lüttwitz. A new government of freedom, order and action has been formed. German honour and honesty shall be restored.

Mutti recounted this to me one afternoon in December 1938. She had just woken up from her afternoon sleep and I had pleaded: 'Please Mutti, before I go to England tell me something about yourself.'
'What would you like to know?'
'What was Berlin like when you were married?'
'Well, we were married on 19 February 1920. After our honeymoon we moved into our flat in Hektorstrasse.'
'Where I was born?'
'Yes, you were born there three years later.'
Mutti carried on with her story. 'Vati's factory was in

Köpenicker Strasse in the east. As the soldiers wouldn't let the bus carry on, Vati took a taxi and in a roundabout way arrived at the factory. Otto Kunze, a trusted worker, greeted him with apprehension.

"You're lucky to have arrived safe and sound."

'Vati replied, "I've nothing to do with politics. Why should anybody harm me?"'

'Kunze replied, "You know Kapp doesn't like Jews."

'"Lots of people don't like us. What are we supposed to do? The government will restore order."

'"The government! You don't seem to know the latest. They've fled."

'"Good God! What will happen now?"

'"We have to do something."

'"What do you think you can do?"

'"Wait and see."

'One of the first things the Kapp government did was issue an order forbidding the distribution of flour to Jewish bakeries for Pesach.'

'Petty thing to do.'

'Yes, they tried to make themselves popular.'

'Well, did they?'

'They miscalculated. The unions declared a general strike. That's what Vati's workers meant. A notice was plastered all over Berlin which said something like this:

'"The military revolt has come! Troops are advancing on Berlin to overthrow the government. We refuse to bend to military compulsion. We will not co-operate with criminals. A thousand times NO. Cease work! Fight to retain the republic!"'

'Factories closed, all public transport stopped. Newspapers stopped publishing. At night Berlin became a ghost town with electricity cut.'

'How did you see?'

'We used candles. The water supply was cut off. Food became short.'

'How did you cook?'

'It was difficult but we wanted the right wing defeated.'

'How did it all end?'

'Kapp didn't expect the workers' resistance. He thought

they would welcome him with open arms. Only four days after he had installed himself in the Wilhelmstrasse he resigned.'

'So that was the end?'

'Unfortunately it wasn't.'

'Did they come back?'

'No. The government returned to Berlin, thanked the unions and asked them to call off the general strike. But Independent Socialists had taken over the unions.'

'Who are they?'

'Today we call them communists, and they called themselves Spartakists.'

'What did they do?'

'They declared a Soviet Republic in Berlin. The government called the police to fight them.'

'Did this affect you?'

'Of course it did. In the morning Vati entered his factory and was greeted by a police officer: "Herr Prager, we have to inform you that we've installed a machine gun on your roof. It is for your protection. The communists are on the other side of the street. They've tried to occupy your factory. We stopped them."

'"What am I supposed to do?"

'"Nothing. Just carry on as usual."

'Suddenly there was a burst of fire. "Down!" somebody shouted. Everybody ducked. The Spartakists had fired at the police.'

'The next day I pleaded with Vati:

'"Please Paul, stay at home today."

'"I must go."

'"But why?"

'"If I don't turn up no work will be done. They'll all go home and God knows when they'll come back."

'"You can't do this to me. We've only been married three weeks."

'"Don't worry. I'll be careful."

'The communists revolt was put down after just one week and normality returned.'

'Did anything happen to Vati?'

'Thank God, no.'

'Are you pleased the communists lost?'

'At the time I was. But now with the Nazis I'm not so sure.'

Childhood

I was born on 26 June 1923. My father was a regular reader of the *Berliner Tageblatt*, and on that day the paper carried two news items which must have caught his eye:

> While Social Democratic youth members were celebrating the summer solstice a group of men wearing swastikas attacked them. One member was seriously wounded and four were slightly wounded.

> Because of repeated anti-Semitic attacks against the aged Herr Fränkel three men have been apprehended. They call themselves National Socialists.

Perhaps this was the reason why, when he registered my birth my father omitted to fill in the 'religion' column. Seventy-two years later the federal German authorities created difficulties when I applied for a restitution pension because I had no proof that I was born a Jew.

Detta Emma was the midwife who brought me into the world and who was called whenever we needed help. Since I was a ten-pound baby, she was called when I was born. She soon became an institution with us and often helped Mutti manage the household. One day guests were expected for dinner. The table was laid carefully and Detta Emma said:

'Peterchen, have your dinner early. If you behave, you can say hello before going to bed.'

The dinner contained spinach which I loathed, but which Mutti made me eat because 'it was good for me'. The plate was put in front of me on the laid table. I ate the meat and potatoes and left the spinach.

'Come on, eat it up. You know Mutti wants you to eat it.' And Detta Emma shoved a spoonful of spinach into my mouth.

The spinach had gone through a mincer. 'This is like castor oil,' I thought. With one regurgitation I spat it out all over the table so that the liquid mass clung to the plates, cutlery, salt cellars and the flowers in the middle. I realized what I had done and started crying.

'The guests will be here any minute!' The table was relaid with a new cloth. 'Now you go to bed at once. No meeting the guests.'

Vati believed that castor oil was good for the constitution. Every weekend he would take a dose, 'to keep me healthy'. Mutti concurred and gave me a spoonful on the slightest pretext. 'Please take just one spoon,' Mutti pleaded. I refused. She came after me with a bottle. I ran to my room and crawled under my bed.

'Come on Peterchen, it is good for you!'

'No! No!' I cried. She threatened me with a stick, and I had to take the stuff.

'Here take these sweets.' They didn't take away the taste and it made me shudder for days.

Though Mutti possessed a cane, she never hit me. I can't remember a single occasion when she threatened me with it, except when I had to swallow castor oil.

* * *

I was seven and was playing in the street. We had started a new hopscotch game when suddenly a girl said:

'Jews are not allowed to play this game. Are you Jewish?'

'What is a Jew?' I asked.

'One who doesn't believe in God.'

'Oh, I'm a Christian.'

'All right then, you can play with us.'

When I recounted this conversation to Mutti, she said nothing, but a few days later Vati explained:

'You are Jewish and we also believe in God.' I was interested and relieved because it enabled me to join in all future games.

* * *

When I was six, Bobby Feistmann was my girlfriend. She lived in our block of flats and our parents were friends. Her big brother was a communist. 'You know, he spends the evenings going to beer cellars beating up Nazis,' Mutti said in a disapproving manner. I had a sneaking admiration for him because my big brother Hans did nothing more exciting than serving in the department store Rosenhain at Christmas.

On my first day at school in April 1929 I arrived with my friend Bobby and my sugar bag. These were cone-shaped, stiff bags filled with sweets which every German schoolchild received on his first day at school. Bobby and I remained friends while at primary school, then we lost touch until we met again during the war at the Free German Youth in London.

The first thing we did was go through registration. Then, the teacher Fraulein Krappatsch asked, 'Can you describe this picture?' It was a picture of Rumpelstiltskin. We had the same picture at home. I put up my hand.

'Yes Peter?'

'It is Rumpelstiltskin.'

'Correct, very good Peter.' I was proud and happy. There were tears from other children but not from me. However, on the second day I suddenly caught fright and ran home in tears.

'What's the matter?' asked Mutti.

'I don't know,' I replied crying.

Mutti brought me back to school. I was always an average scholar, never brilliant. If there had been an 11+ exam I would have failed, but in those days grammar school education was not free, so there was little pressure.

* * *

In 1930 Mutti divorced Vati and the following year she married Onkel Franz. Six years later Vati remarried and I had now, in addition to a mother and father, a stepfather and stepmother. This did not worry me, but as I lived with Mutti the confusion of surnames sometimes caused me embarrassment.

After Mutti's marriage she said, 'Peter, from now on you mustn't visit our bedroom any more.' I didn't like this and one morning charged into their bedroom. Onkel Franz rushed out and gave me a real hiding. Somehow after that there was a gulf between Mutti and myself. However, my relationship with Onkel Franz remained very friendly and he never laid hands on me again.

* * *

Jews as Outcasts

'Come Peter, let's go to the parade,' Vati said on Sunday mornings. I looked forward to this. Vati took me to the Tomb of the Unknown Soldier and we watched the changing of the guard. Then both of us, together with hundreds of spectators, marched with the soldiers behind the army band through the Brandenburg Gate. The traffic stopped, people looked at us, and I felt exhilarated, while Vati thought of the good old times.

'Hitler has won the provincial elections. On Sunday (because of street riots) I could not go by bus to Vati but had to take the overhead railway. The police were on emergency duty and the soldiers marched without music, so that we had to go home without seeing anything. The police carried rifles.' I was nine when I wrote this to Mutti who was taking the cure for her rheumatism at Bad Pistyan.

One day in the same year, one rather tough-looking boy at my primary school seemed to go berserk. His parents were known to be Nazis. He shouted, 'When Hitler comes to power he'll turn everything upside-down'. And he hit everybody and overturned desks.

When I told Mutti she said, 'Yes, that's what it's going to be like'.

Circus Bush had its permanent home at the back of Monbijou Platz where Vati lived after the divorce. He took me there every time their programme changed. I remember one act: Siegmund Breitbart, the Iron King. Six men placed a huge wooden board over his outstretched body, and a lorry drove over the board without in any way harming him. He bent iron bars and tore iron chains with his bare hands.

Vati recounted to me: 'I remember 1923, the year you were born, there were anti-Jewish riots in the Scheunenviertel, the Jewish east end. Did you know Breitbart is Jewish?'

'No, I didn't. He doesn't look it.'

'Well he is.'

'Tell me about the riots.'

'Breitbart was there and he beat up several rioters. He challenged them: "If you want to match your strength against mine, come next Sunday at three o'clock to the circus." The contest was well advertised, so the circus was sold out. Most spectators merely wanted to see a sensational act, but the audience also contained a large number of Jew baiters and many Jews from the Scheunenviertel. The spectacle began. The announcer asked: "Will anybody come forward to match their strength with Siegmund Breitbart?" Three of the ex-rioters whom Breitbart had man-handled came forward and entered the ring. An anvil had been placed in the middle of the stage. They were told to take an axe and hit the anvil with all their strength, with Breitbart lying underneath. Furiously they hit harder and harder. The anvil had been placed on a large wooden board and hitting it merely spread the force of the impact over the entire board and therefore couldn't harm Breitbart. It's an old circus trick.'

'Isn't this cheating?'

'Not really. Only stupid people don't know about it.'

'What happened next?'

'The more strength they used the more exhausted they became. Finally they gave up. Breitbart appeared from underneath the board, pushed them contemptuously aside and, amid tremendous applause walked off the stage.'

This was a triumph for the Jews, wasn't it?'

* * *

In 1936, the first Sunday in the month was cheap day at the Berlin Zoo, and during the summer months Vati took me there regularly. Near the entrance was the newly built elephant compound without bars. A baby elephant had just been born and people were queuing up to see it. Behind the elephants were the monkeys and apes, and I spent hours looking at their performing tricks. One day I found an especially large crowd in the area where the baby elephant used to be but the elephants had gone.

'Look, what's there!' I shouted excitedly. A family of Negroes was housed in the compound. The men were lounging about while the women were cooking a meal. The description on the notice read: 'This tribe comes from Tanganyika, formerly German East Africa'. These Africans seemed to be happy and contented and no doubt thought they were very well off. They received shelter and food in return for being stared at by white spectators.

Most Germans had never seen a Negro and they were a sensation. 'Daddy, don't they look like gorillas?' A little boy next to me said this to his father who was in a stormtrooper's uniform. As a 13 year old boy it seemed to me that these black people represented an early stage in the development of the human species. They had not yet advanced to the level of the white man. The fact that they were housed next to the apes drove home the point which the government wanted us to learn.

* * *

It is 1937 and I am travelling from Halensee to Charlottenburg by overhead railway. My carriage is almost empty. Then a man enters and sits opposite me.

'Hello, young man'. I don't reply.

'You're not very friendly. What's the matter?' I look away. He moves closer to me and starts touching my bare legs. As the train enters Charlottenburg station I rush out. The man follows me. I run to the station master's office.

'This man is following me. Please help!'

'He's crazy. I'm not following him.' But the station master directs both of us into his office.

'I don't know what this boy wants. I haven't done anything.'

'He touched my legs.'

'Nonsense! He's a liar.'

'We'll see about that,' says the station master. 'Your identity paper!' The man shows his papers. The official takes down all the details and gives them to me.

'Take this to your parents. Tell them to go to the police. Now run off. I'll keep him here until you've disappeared.'

'Let's wait till Onkel Franz comes home and see what he says,' says Mutti.

'The station master never asked you for your papers?' asks Onkel Franz.

'No. He didn't.'

'That means he doesn't know you're Jewish. The trouble is, nowadays, no judge will find in favour of a Jew against an Aryan. It would be best to forget all about it.'

I'm beginning to learn that we are outcasts.

2 The Prager Family

Vati was smoking a pipe. Well, he wasn't really smoking. There was no tobacco in the pipe because he had no money.

'Tell me about the factory,' I said. We were sitting in our furnished room in Cricklewood. It was a Sunday afternoon in 1943 and the rain was pelting against the window.

'You see, Peter, we were one of the oldest Jewish families in Prussia. In 1812 Jews were given citizenship and with it the right to move about and to trade and manufacture. Your great-grandfather was a master carpenter and he took advantage of this. He moved from Silesia to Berlin. In 1821 he founded a suitcase factory. As you know it existed until the Nazis took it over in 1936.'

Vati continued: 'Your grandfather had two children, Onkel Georg and me. We were assimilated and celebrated Christmas rather than Chanukah. The whole family would gather under the Christmas tree and sing Christmas carols.'

He carried on: 'I had piano lessons with my friend Bruno Schlesinger. We made good progress but Bruno was so much better. I couldn't keep up with him. The piano teacher asked: "Will you two play before an invited audience?" I agreed reluctantly because I felt exceedingly awkward playing with such a superb pianist. I was relieved when the teacher said: "From now on you'll have separate lessons." Later, when Bruno studied music I went into the family business. We saw less of each other. Eventually, we only met after concerts when I went backstage to exchange a few words with Bruno Walter, as he now called himself.'

'Did you see him in England?'

'I didn't arrive until 1 September 1939. By then he'd left for the States. Now I can only listen to him on the wireless.'

'You still like playing the piano, don't you?'

'Yes, I do, when I have the opportunity. I love

improvisations. Anyway, you know I was in England when I was about your age.'

'Tell me about it.'

'As part of my education my mother sent me to London to learn English. I was apprenticed to a jewellers in Bond Street.'

'Where did you live?'

'Chalk Farm.'

'Did you enjoy your time in England?'

'I loved it. I did a lot of swimming and riding, and I was a member of the Thames Rowing Club. I never wanted to leave.'

'Why did you?'

'I was called up to do my national service.'

* * *

'Tell me more about the factory.'

'In 1897 we were appointed manufacturer to the Imperial Court and the Court of Prussia. We made suitcases for the army and for the Kaiser, on one occasion even for Queen Victoria.'

'Did you ever meet her?'

'No, of course not. We got the order through her agent.'

'Was the Kaiser friendly to Jews?'

'He had no objections to doing business with Jews but he would not let us become officers in the army even though we were conscripted like all Germans. Actually I know the Kaiser liked Jews. He played skat [a card game] regularly with some Jewish businessmen. I was trying to get on the reserve list in case one of the players fell ill. Unfortunately the war broke out, I was called up, and bang went my hopes of playing skat with the Kaiser.'

* * *

'Tell me what you did in the war.'

'I took part in the advance through Belgium. As German troops marched through Belgian villages, mothers stood holding their babies tight, crying: "Please spare our babies." I couldn't understand their anxieties until I came across an English newspaper depicting German soldiers spiking

11

Belgian babies. They tried to arouse anti-German hatred with these lies. This British propaganda had unfortunate consequences for us Jews when the Nazis came to power. I was struck by people's disbelief when I told them what happened to me at Sachsenhausen. The public had been fooled during the First World War and they were reluctant to believe such stories again.'

'How did you become an officer?'

'Because of the war Jews were allowed promotion. You could only become an officer when elected unanimously by all the officers of the regiment. There was one anti-Semite in my regiment. He was sent on leave, so that I could be elected. I finished the war as a captain and won the Hanseaten Kreuz for bravery.'

* * *

When during the 1930 depression all workers' wages were cut, my father refused to cut wages in his own factory. He said: 'My workers are skilled craftsmen. I can't expect them to work for less money.'

One of the firm's specialities was a trunk which could be mounted on the back of a car. In the early 1930s streamlined cars with boots were designed, which could only take small suitcases, but my father did not switch production. I remember once when we wanted a taxi, he walked along the taxi rank until he found an old-fashioned taxi without a boot. He climbed into the taxi and said to the driver in front who was driving a newly designed car: 'I always prefer taxis without a boot. They're safer. They have better balance'. He thought this would help to maintain the old system. He went bankrupt at the first whiff of the depression.

* * *

Five years after his divorce from Mutti he married again. Now I had a step-mother, Tante Trude, and he moved to her flat. Tante Trude was a rich widow and she was able to send money illegally to England, but not enough to obtain a visa for both of them. She decided that Vati should go to England first and try to organize her emigration later on. During the pogrom only men had been arrested. But in 1942 Vati received a Red Cross letter stating she had moved to an unknown address. It was Auschwitz.

Vati's life had been a failure, although he didn't give the impression of being cast down by it. He had inherited a successful business, but saw it going bankrupt even before the Nazis gave it the final push. His personal life had been completely disrupted. In England he was a night watchman, but I never heard him complain: he took his menial employment in England as seriously as his prestigious business in Germany.

In his eagerness to fit in at his new job he went to extraordinary lengths. At Christmas all the night watchmen of the district held a dance. Afterwards Vati bitterly complained to me: 'Bill's wife wouldn't dance with me. What have I done to annoy her? I can't understand it.'

I had met Bill and his wife. He was a broad bulky man who had always been very friendly to Vati. His wife was lightly built, youngish and quite pretty. I said: 'Surely, it was just an oversight.'

'No, it wasn't. It was deliberate.'

'How do you know?'

'She looked away and pretended not to hear when I asked her.'

'What are you going to do about it?'

'Next Saturday I'm going to see my friend Joe to ask his advice.'

'How will that help?'

'I'll tell him what happened to find out whether he thinks I've done something to annoy her'.

The meeting was held.

'What did Joe say?'

'Joe said to me, "Isn't it true that you met the Kaiser?" I said "yes". Then he said, "Didn't you make suitcases for Queen Victoria?" I answered, "Well, so what?" Then he just remarked, "And you still worry that Bill's wife wouldn't dance with you?" Then he left.'

'Are you satisfied?'

'I have to be. I still think she should have made some friendly gesture.'

Later he sent her a bunch of flowers to show that he was still willing.

* * *

Vati died of a stroke in 1946. I remember him as somebody who never seemed to get angry and always smiled. He had an equable temperament and gave the impression that he was without emotion. But he had loved Mutti and the divorce shook him to the core. This shock made him even more diffident about showing his feelings. I have inherited some of my father's character and probably would feel better if I were able to show my emotions more instead of bottling them up. But it's difficult to alter one's personality. Vati loved me and imagined he was looking after me when we were living together during the war, never realizing that mentally I was completely divorced from him: I told him of plans but never asked him for advice. Vati was an intelligent and upright person and I liked him very much but was unable to love him. When I heard of Vati's death, while serving in Germany, I felt sorry but I could not feel a personal loss. I still often feel guilty about it.

Onkel Georg and Tante Cläre

Onkel Georg was Vati's brother. He was a master carpenter in their factory and was factory manager while Vati was concerned with the business side.

I visited Onkel Georg and Tante Cläre regularly. I was always greeted with, 'Hello Peter, sit down and eat with us'. He was a little, thin man whilst Tante Cläre though also short was slightly thickset. Onkel Georg had diabetes and he had to eat frequent and large meals. Like Vati he had served an apprenticeship in England, so when the Nazis took the business away he earned his living teaching English. They had three children, two of whom died in infancy and the third in an accident on a mountain climbing expedition. I was always amazed at how well they took their misfortunes. They were constantly joking and their home was full of laughter.

When the firm L. Prager went bankrupt, their entire

furniture went as a surety to the creditors. The creditors were their friends, the Johns, who let them retain the flat and household belongings.

The John Family

When Vati went sailing in his yacht on the Müggelsee, he often went with his closest friend, John. He was tall and broadly built. When he spoke he had a loud and resonant voice. When he called his wife, Anna, the sound reverberated like a loudspeaker throughout the house. He was an accountant and had rented an island on the River Spree.

On one occasion John said to Vati: 'Ask Peter to stay with us for a weekend. He'll enjoy the swimming.' I was delighted and looked forward to the trip. The river contained mussels, and the Johns caught them and ate them as a delicacy. On the Saturday night I was there, mussels were caught, tipped into boiling water and then distributed around the party. Nucky, the daughter, said: 'Here Peter, have one.' I was supposed to like them. I tried to swallow but found that they made me feel sick. We were having our meal on the veranda, and it was dark. Every time I was given a mussel I put it in my mouth, went to the other end of the veranda and spat it out into the garden. Then I rejoined the others.

'Did you like them?' asked Nucky.

'Yes, of course.'

* * *

One day John's employer asked him to falsify his accounts in order to avoid tax payments. This he did, but the authorities found out, he was charged with fraud and sent to prison. As a result most of his friends left him, but not Vati or Onkel Georg. They stuck to him through thick and thin.

'True friendship must withstand all adversity,' Vati explained to me.

* * *

John was attracted to the Nazis as soon as he read about the abortive Nazi *Putsch* in Munich in 1923. Like so many Germans, he was appalled by the harsh treatment the new democratic Germany had received from the Allies, and he thought Hitler would regenerate Germany. When Goebbels became Gauleiter of Berlin with the object of winning the capital for Nazism, John was one of the first to join the Party. He now owned a beer cellar which became one of the rallying points for the stormtroopers. However, he actively opposed the anti-Jewish campaigns and regularly spoke against anti-Semitism at party meetings. 'Surely we all know that this anti-Jewish talk is all nonsense. Jews are just as good as we are.' His pleas were met with incomprehension by the stormtroopers. The Nazi hierarchy ignored him and then pushed him aside. They dared not attack him because members of the Old Guard were specially honoured and cited as examples to be followed.

When Vati was forced to sell the firm to a Gentile, John immediately bought it so that Vati and Onkel Georg could carry on as usual. The Nazis did not approve and the factory had to be sold again to more reliable Nazis. Within two years these new owners went into fraudulent bankruptcy. The machines were sold and the firm ceased to exist.

* * *

John died in 1936 of a heart attack. I recollect when it happened. It was a Sunday and I was staying with Vati. The phone rang, Vati lifted the receiver and turned white.

'It's bad news.' He turned to Tante Trude. 'John is dead.'

Tante Trude sat down and wept. Mutti cried too when I told her. The protector of the family had gone. John had decreed that Onkel Georg should hold the funeral oration but the Nazis had different ideas. They could not make use of him during his lifetime because of his pro-Jewish views, but they could utilize his death for propaganda purposes. John was buried with full Nazi honours and held as a shining example to German youth. A notice to this effect appeared in the *Völkischer Beobachter* (the official organ of the Nazi Party).

John's widow and his daughter Nucky remained friends of the family. They gave much support to Onkel Georg and Tante

Cläre until they were deported to Theresienstadt. They accompanied them to Wannsee Station, the deportation centre, and gave them plenty of food parcels on the way, a courageous action at a time when Goebbels had expressly forbidden the showing of any sympathy towards Jews. The food parcels were of particular value to Onkel Georg because of his diabetes. It was of no avail; he died on the journey. Tante Cläre did not come back. After the war Nucky married a British soldier and went to live in England.

3   The Blumenthal Family

My grandfather was a tall, lean and energetic man who, though in his eighties, would still climb stairs two steps at a time. His strong personality dominated the entire family; he was a Victorian dictator whom everybody held in awe. But he had a soft spot for me, and called me Peterchen. The 'chen' is an endearing diminutive in German and I was the only member of his large family so called. My first visit to a synagogue was with him on Kol Nidrei. Suddenly the congregation fell to its knees, and Grandfather explained to me: 'We Jews don't normally kneel before God. We do it once on Yom Kippur to repent for our sins.'

Grandfather came from Bromberg in Poznan, now in Poland. My mother loved to talk about her father. It was 1937, she rested on the sofa and related: 'You know, he was a good Prussian, proud of his sharp shooting.' In fact he kept his log book all his life to show what a good shot he was, and 50 years later I went through my mother's memorabilia and found his 1872 log book. My mother continued: 'He was called up to fight in the Franco-Prussian war in 1870.'

'Did he fight at Sedan?'

'Yes he did, and he was proud of it.'

'Was he one of the soldiers who took Napoleon prisoner?'

'No, but he did take part in the siege of Paris.'

'Tell me about it.'

'The German soldiers were starving just like the Parisians.'

'I suppose, they had to catch rabbits in the fields.'

'Worse than that. They ate rats. It was horrible. He says that's why he still has stomach ulcers today.'

'And what did he do after the war?'

'Before the war he walked the streets of Bromberg with his cart selling coal. Well, he thought he could do better, so he started his own coal business. He bought coal from the

Silesian mines, hired boats to transport it along the River Oder to Berlin and then sold it to Berlin coal merchants. We buy our coal from merchants who have been supplied by him.'

'Do we get it cheaper?'

'Of course not. Recently the firm celebrated its 55th birthday. It's now the biggest coal business in eastern Germany.'

'How did he come to live in Berlin?'

'In 1919 the entire area became Polish. As a good German he moved to Berlin.'

Mutti's stories about Grandfather thrilled me. He was lucky to die in 1934 and miss the horrors that were to come. At that time we still thought Hitler's regime would not last.

I wanted to know about my uncles: 'Tell me about Onkel Benno.'

'Grandfather made the decisions about the future of all his children – they had no say in the matter. He decided that Benno was to become legal adviser to the business. He was made to study law; in the event he failed his legal exams three times.'

'Was Grandfather annoyed?'

'I should say so. He accused him of being not sufficiently keen. This was probably true. He passed the fourth time but was so hopeless at law that Grandfather made him the firm's representative instead. You know he is rather plump.'

'Yes, I know. Everybody calls him Dicker.' (In German this means 'fatso' but is a form of endearment.)

'He never married. He is the darling of the family. He wouldn't hurt a fly. I love him dearly.'

In 1943 he was deported to Theresienstadt. He wrote a postcard on the day of his deportation. It read: 'Dear sister, a farewell greeting. Yours Benno.' His trembling hand could not manage his usual regular handwriting. The second card was sent by Onkel Benno on 10 January 1944: 'Dearest sister. I have waited many weeks for news but at last your parcel and card arrived. Many thanks. I am pleased you are both well. I feel fairly satisfactory. Many regards to you, Franz, all friends and above all Grossmutti [mother of Franz]. Yours Benno.' It took five months for this card to arrive. By then he had been sent to Auschwitz.

(After the war Mutti grieved over Onkel Benno's death more than anyone else's. Like millions of others he was missing in 1945, and Mutti hoped against hope that he might emerge among the very few survivors. While I was in the army I received notification from the International Red Cross that he had perished in Auschwitz. I was afraid to tell Mutti and gave the Red Cross letter to Onkel Jean, so that Benno's fate would dawn only slowly on her.)

Mutti continued: 'Brother Paul seemed to be brighter, so Father made him manager of the coal business. He managed it so well that Grandfather could retire early to nurse his ulcers. Paul and Lotte had a daughter, Marion, your cousin. As you know he is rich. You've been to his mansion in Schmargendorf. He gives parties and likes to stand at the porch to receive visitors. When I married Onkel Franz and introduced him for the first time, Franz entered the house, sniffed, looked around and said, "it stinks of money." '

As she told me this I broke out laughing, but Mutti said: 'I didn't like him saying that. After all, Paul is my brother. Franz was never invited again.'

They did invite me at times. I was surprised that their living room had no clock. 'With all their money, can't they afford a clock?' I asked Mutti.

'Onkel Paul and Tante Lotte are very hospitable people. When they invite friends, they don't want them to see a clock, in case this causes them to leave early.'

After the Nazis had taken away their firm, they had to do forced labour at the Siemens factory in Berlin. Mutti recounted: 'One day on the way to work, Tante Lotte fell and broke her leg. As soon as passers-by saw the yellow star they wouldn't help. She lay on the road for hours until Onkel Paul was able to get her to hospital.

When they received their final deportation orders Lotte distributed their valuables among their Gentile friends, including an antique wardrobe which she sent to Marion's former nanny in the country. She gave everybody my parent's address. Tante Lotte was quite sure she'd return to claim her belongings, but Paul foresaw their fate. Their destination too was Auschwitz.

After the war the nanny contacted Mutti because she

wanted to return the wardrobe. Mutti wrote and told her to keep the wardrobe as a memento of Paul and Lotte. But the nanny said she couldn't keep someone else's valuables and the wardrobe was sent back. None of the other recipients returned anything.

Onkel Jean

'Now I'll tell you about Onkel Jean, my favourite brother,' said Mutti. 'He's nearest my age and we always played together. There was one incident I'll never forget. I was seven and he was five, and he couldn't learn to distinguish left from right. So one day I jammed his left thumb in the door. He shrieked with pain until I let the door go. "This is left," I said, pointing to his bruised thumb.'

'You were terribly cruel.'

'I was only seven and didn't realize what damage I might have done. But he forgave me and we were always close. He longed to be a violinist but Father decided he was to become a doctor. He set up a stiff resistance but was forced to go to medical college, and when he was there he went to violin classes. When Father found out he threatened to cut off his meagre allowance. Jean's dispute with Father left a bitter taste all his life.'

I knew Onkel Jean better than the other brothers because he and his wife managed to escape to England in 1939. The General Medical Council had a rule, that only doctors with a degree from a British or British Empire university were allowed to practise in Britain. The Home Office had another rule, which stated that no foreigner could obtain a labour permit if there was an unemployed British subject who could do the job. With more than two million unemployed there wasn't much chance for Onkel Jean.

As the war progressed the labour situation began to change, and in January 1940 he became bakery assistant at the ABC factory in Camden Town. A few weeks later he saw an advertisement: 'Crane drivers required. Training given.' He applied and was given the job. He was remarkably unsuccessful and made the cranes fly in unexpected directions.

One day his foreman approached him. 'I hear you're a doctor, is this true?'

'Yes it is, but as an alien I'm not allowed to practise in this country.'

'Would you like to run our first aid post?'

'Certainly!' Onkel Jean's face lit up.

The next day the foreman arrived with a strained expression. 'Unfortunately I've been told you can't do first aid in this country without a first aid course. We don't recognize your medical degree. Do you mind going on the course?'

'Not at all.' He was happy to do something in connection with health. On 24 July 1940 he passed his test in First Aid. His first aid certificate even omitted the title 'doctor' from his name, a further ignominy he had to bear. Glad as he was to be in England, this was a bitter experience.

As British casualties mounted, the General Medical Council issued a new regulation stating that refugee doctors could act as assistant doctors in a medical practice provided they were under the supervision of a British doctor. Only when Aneuran Bevan became Minister of Health after the war was Onkel Jean finally permitted to run his own practice. This he did successfully for another 20 years in Shepherd's Bush.

* * *

Onkel Jean had an atrocious accent which he blamed on Onkel Georg who had taught him English. Forty years' residence in England did not improve it and I often wondered how his patients understood him, because he pronounced everything as if it were German.

We visited him regularly with our children. 'Peter, I don't like the table manners of your children. Look! Alison is grabbing the food with her fingers!'

'Onkel Jean, she's only two.'

'That has nothing to do with it. If you don't start early they'll never learn and they won't thank you for it.'

'Don't worry, when they're grown up they will have learnt how to eat.'

'I suppose you think because I've no children I don't know how children should behave.' Although that was precisely what I thought I made no reply.

At that moment Hazel, my elder daughter aged five, got up from her chair, climbed on to Onkel Jean and grabbed his glasses.

'You see, Peter, that happens because you don't teach them any discipline. The trouble with you is you believe in these new ideas of bringing up children and this is the result. What silly books on child psychology are you reading?'

'I'm not reading any. We just bring up our children according to common sense.'

'Oh, so you think I've no common sense?'

'I haven't said that. But we are the parents and we like to bring up our children our way.' After this discussion we didn't speak to each other for an entire year. In the end there was a reconciliation – after all, he was the only member of my parents' generation still alive.

* * *

One day Onkel Jean phoned me and said: 'I have a terrible pain in my shoulder.'

'It must be rheumatism,' I replied.

'It probably is. Well, goodbye.'

He became more explicit with my brother with whom he was closer. 'Look after Annie,' he said to Hans the same evening, 'I think this is the end'.

The same night he died of a heart attack.

Tante Annie

Onkel Jean's wife Annie was dismissed from her post at the Preussische Staatsbank in 1933. With a number of other women, she decided to organize the rescue of Jewish children to Palestine and she became co-founder of the Children and Youth Aliya. When the organization's headquarters was transferred from Berlin to London she became its organizing secretary, a post she retained until her retirement.

She was the only member of the family who had succeeded in escaping from Germany in time: her mother, sister, brother and sister-in-law all perished in Auschwitz. Her hatred of everything German was absolute. She loved German sausages but would only eat them if they had been made outside Germany. When she was ill, I brought her orange juice that had been bottled in Germany. Furiously, she returned it to me, saying, 'You know I don't take anything German.'

During her final illness she suddenly refused to have a bath and two nurses were unable to undress her. She explained: 'This reminds me of Auschwitz. People had to undress thinking they were going to have a shower but then gas came out of the taps.' The nurses made no further attempt to bathe her.

Ludwig Patschke

'Peter, I want you to meet Rainer. He is an excellent chess player. He'll teach you the game. Meanwhile I'll examine his father.'

'Are you fond of music?' Rainer asked.

'Yes, but I can't play an instrument.'

'Dr Blumenthal is teaching me the violin.'

Rainer was the son of Ludwig Patschke, who was a patient of Onkel Jean in Berlin. He was unemployed but Onkel Jean befriended him and, as they had similar interests, they became close friends.

* * *

A telephone call from Patschke on 9 November 1938: 'Jean, I've just seen what is happening in the streets. Come at once to my flat. You don't want the Gestapo to get you. When things quieten down you can go home.'

After three nights Onkel Jean returned to his flat. 'You've saved me from Sachsenhausen.'

* * *

In 1939 Patschke visited Hans in London. 'Patschke, here is a letter from home. It looks as though it is from your wife. Goodness, you're turning white. What's the matter?'

'It's a summons to the Gestapo.'

'I wonder what they want.'

'I'm not going. I'll stay in England.'

'The Home Office won't give you a permit to stay.'

'I'll go to the Quakers for advice.'

At the Quaker office he was told: 'We've had a number of cases like this. In our experience, when you don't turn up for the interview, your wife and possibly also your son will be arrested.'

'That means I'll have to go back.'

The interview took place at the Gestapo headquarters on Albrecht Strasse.

'We have information that you sheltered a Jew on 9, 10 and 11 November.'

'It was my doctor. He came to me for help and I could not refuse.'

'We have also been informed that your son has played with a Jewish child.'

'He did. While the doctor examined me Rainer played with his nephew.'

'We have to tell you that this is un-German behaviour. If you persist in this activity you will have to have a spell in a concentration camp.'

* * *

'And what lies have they told you at school today?' Patschke would greet his son every day and then correct any misinformation.

One day Rainer brought a letter home. 'It's from my headmaster. Have I done anything wrong?'

'No, no. He just wants to see me.'

At the interview, the headmaster confronted Patschke: 'Last week our biology teacher gave the children a lesson on race as prescribed in the national curriculum. The next day Rainer told the teacher that he was wrong, that the Aryan race is not superior and that Jews are not inferior. Did you tell him this?'

'I did. All I meant to say was that people can have different views.'

'If you contradict our teaching again I will have to report you to the appropriate authorities.'

* * *

Patschke was an army captain during the war and was put in charge of a British POW camp. He gave the prisoners the latest news from the BBC regularly. He said to one of his sergeants, pointing to his Nazi Party membership badge: 'If I were you, I'd hide that thing. Soon you'll be frightened to admit that you've ever been a member.' The sergeant denounced him and Captain Patschke was immediately suspended. He was to be court-martialled for sedition. His defence lawyer told him: 'Unfortunately you'll be found guilty and sentenced to death. All I can do for you is to postpone the trial. With luck the war will be over soon.'

It was December 1944. Rainer received his call up papers. His father said: 'You're not going into the army. We'll travel to the Sudeten. In the present chaos nobody will find us.' Berlin was in ruins, the railway lines to and from Berlin were constantly bombed and the postal service was completely disorganised.

Ludwig Patschke's court-martial was fixed for 10 May. Germany surrendered on 8 May.

4   Mutti and Bruder Hans

Mutti's story

'I was born on 21 March 1888 in Bromberg. This is in the province of Poznan and is now Polish. I was the only girl and Grossvati was much more indulgent towards me than towards his sons. I was always grieved about the way he treated Jean my favourite brother. I went to the Höhere Töchterschule, an academy for young ladies.'

Later, Onkel Jean told me: 'When Mutti went for walks through the town, people gazed at her. She was tall, blue eyed with light brown hair. "Why do people keep on looking at me? What's wrong with me?" she asked. I told her she was the prettiest girl in town. "Don't be silly," she said and she blushed. But others agreed with me. She was known as the beauty of Bromberg.'

Mutti continued: 'In spite of Grossvati's indulgence towards me, he insisted on whom I was to marry.'

'Surely, you were able to choose.'

'You forget, in those days, girls of 17 didn't choose husbands. This was done by our parents. Grossvati chose a rich country doctor.'

'Was he Hans' father?'

'Yes, he was.'

'Did you love him?' I asked.

'I don't think love came into it. He was quite good looking. Unfortunately Felix had a secret. He was a morphia addict.'

'Terrible. How did he become addicted?'

'As a doctor it was easy for him to get hold of the drug. When nearby chemists became suspicious of the number of morphia prescriptions he was writing, he sent our maid all over town to chemists who didn't know him.'

'Why didn't you stop him?'

'You don't understand the times we were living in. We had been taught absolute obedience to our husband.'

'Surely not in a case like this.'

'Well, I didn't know what to do. When he was craving the drug he had violent fits of temper. I felt helpless. On one occasion he chased me and your brother with a knife. I locked the two of us in a room. Then the doorbell rang. I crept out and it was Onkel Jean.'

'That was lucky.'

'Yes it was. It was a surprise visit; he had a bag of sweets for Hans. He was stunned at what he saw and asked what was going on. I told him that Felix wasn't feeling well, that it was morphia.

'Jean immediately grasped the situation, and said: "Has this happened before? You must come with me! Don't pack, just bring what you need for the night."

'The next time I saw Felix he was in a home. He died soon afterwards.

'At that time Ibsen's play *A Doll's House* was showing in town. It was a revelation to most of us women, a bombshell. You know, it sounds unbelievable but there were married women who committed suicide after seeing this play. They felt trapped in marriage, unable to run away like Nora. My reaction was, "Never again. I will never again let myself suffer in marriage as I did then."'

* * *

'Then I moved to a flat in Berlin. When Hans was 12, I felt that he needed a father, so I looked around. I said to him: "Hans, I'm going to invite a number of men here. You must tell me whether you like them or not."

'"Why?"

'"I want to get married. But I promise, I won't marry anyone you don't like." A number of men appeared on the scene. Then came your father. Hans had a conversation with him.

'"What's your hobby?" Hans asked.

'"Sailing," he answered.

'"Where do you sail?"

'"I have a sailing yacht on the Müggelsee. I go there at weekends. I can take you along if you like." That sealed the deal as far as Hans was concerned. "I like him best," he said.

'Paul had other attractions. He was a factory owner appointed by the Kaiser, with showrooms at Unter den Linden. The Kaiser had abdicated but this didn't matter in Prussia and your father had a good business reputation. As soon as we were married we were to move to a luxury flat along the Kurfürstendamm. But the inflation of 1923 ruined everything: the yacht was sold, the firm went bankrupt. We never saw the luxury flat. The firm struggled on but during the 1929 depression we went broke again.

Then Onkel Franz appeared on the scene. He was dissatisfied with his wife. We fell in love. Your father couldn't earn a living so I had to go out to work. I never loved your father and, remembering Nora, I divorced him. The rest you know.'

Growing up with Mutti

In 1930, when I returned from my usual summer holidays with Detta Emma to our flat in Berlin, Mutti said to me: 'Vati doesn't live here any more. He has moved nearer his factory. But you can see him every weekend.' This I did.

The following year while visiting Detta Emma in Caminchen, she said: 'Is it true that your parents have divorced?'

'No. Vati has moved nearer his factory.'

I asked Mutti: 'Have you divorced Vati?'

'Yes I have. But that won't make any difference to you. You can see him just as much as before'.

Mutti married Onkel Franz in the same year.

Though I liked Onkel Franz, Mutti's change of husband made me cling more to her. It made me adopt her beliefs unquestioningly. Vati and Onkel Franz were outsiders, what really mattered were her ideas. My brother Hans had left home, so there were just the two of us and my attachment to her was extreme. She caught pneumonia and in those days, before penicillin, there was a crisis point when she might have died. I was devastated, I couldn't imagine life without her.

When she convalesced I said to her: 'Wouldn't it have been nice if I could have married you?' I was 13.

She answered: 'You know, I wanted you to be a girl.' I felt flattered. Her attitude brought about an ambivalence in me towards my own sexuality. It was only when I was in England and completely separated from her – when I was 15 – that my normal masculine sexuality asserted itself.

* * *

When Mutti was 35 she began to suffer from rheumatoid arthritis which in the course of time crippled her to such an extent that she could only walk with a stick. Her right hand was so deformed that she had to shake hands with the left. Every summer she went to a different spa hoping to find some relief from her illness, but nothing worked. Onkel Jean, a doctor, had to watch his own sister become a cripple without being able to help.

As her limbs became deformed she suffered intolerable pain. She cried out at night and woke up Onkel Franz. To allow him to sleep she decided to spend the nights in the living room on a couch. This was next to my room, and I woke up every night and heard her walking up and down, sighing and groaning. It left a terrible impression on me. I loved Mutti and her suffering caused me great pain and anguish. She was an avid reader but couldn't hold a book, so I made a bookstand in the woodwork class at school. I was proud of my achievement because I was so poor at handiwork.

Then Mutti was urged by a homeopath to have a salt-free diet. Onkel Franz decreed: 'No more cooking with salt.' I had read in books of discovery that Africans deprived of salt would exchange valuables for salt and then eat it by the spoonful. After a few months of a salt-free diet I longed for salt like those Africans. When I came home from school I made myself sandwiches by spreading bread thickly with salt. To me it was a delicacy.

Our flat was three flights up and there wasn't a lift. It was difficult for Mutti to go shopping, so she made a shopping list for me every day and said: 'After homework get me one pound of lean mince meat and eggs.' There was a shortage of eggs but no rationing scheme, so I went from shop to shop and asked for eggs. When the shopkeeper knew me he gave me two or three. I hated buying the meat. The butcher would show me the mince and ask me if it was alright. I said it was, but when I got home Mutti told me off: 'You're stupid. Can't you see all the fat in this mince?'

* * *

When I returned in 1946 our relationship was reversed. Instead of Mutti looking after me, I looked after her. The war years had made her so frail that she could not have withstood the post-war starvation period without my help. Now she knew nothing about me, nor did I feel the need to tell her anything about myself and my girlfriends. I had grown away from her.

When Onkel Franz died, Hans and I brought her to England. She died a year later of cancer.

Bruder Hans

He was my 'big brother'. When I was a toddler he didn't like it that I slept in his room. Later he told me: 'You woke me up in the mornings, standing in your cot making a noise fluttering your eyelashes.' He was 13 years older than me and I was proud of him – 'Bruder Hans says I've grown several centimetres in the last few weeks.' 'Bruder Hans is taking me for a walk.' 'Bruder Hans can play chess against himself.' He always adopted a protective attitude towards me which was alright while I was young, but became burdensome when I was an adult and particularly after I was married. Throughout he tried to tell me how to live my life.

* * *

In 1931 Hans was 21 and came into his father's money. Mutti told him to use it wisely, but Hansn had other ideas.

'Why should I work when I can live on the interest?' Hans thought. 'But I must be careful with it. Thank God I've got a large family. I'll invite myself to meals as often as possible. I'll start with Onkel Paul and Tante Lotte. They always give big parties. They won't mind.'

'Don't you think you should study something?' Mutti asked.

'I've no time. I've got a girlfriend.' Her name was Gretel and she wasn't Jewish. This obliged him to leave for England as soon as the Nazis came to power. According to the Nürnberg Laws of 1935 sex between Jews and Aryans had been forbidden. He had to pay an emigration tax of 75 per cent to get his money transferred to sterling – 'crazy' my mother called it. 'He should have stayed here and taken a decent job.' Soon there were no jobs for Jews and the emigration tax was raised to 90 per cent. Finally Jews were only allowed to take out 10 Marks and no country would accept penniless Jews.

After the pogrom Mutti wrote to Hans: 'Please can you find a family for Peter? Life in Berlin has become impossible.' He did and that's how I came to England.

In 1940 he was interned like all of us. 'I must do something to feed Gretel and the baby,' he told me. 'I'd better volunteer for the army. There's no other way.'

He loathed the army discipline, in particular the marching exercises. He told the quarter-master he couldn't wear boots as his feet hurt. He was given another pair.

'I've had enough,' he remarked to me when on leave, and the following week he reported sick, telling the medical orderly that he could not walk. He was put into a military hospital.

'What's your illness?' I wrote to him.

'Flat feet,' he wrote back. 'I'm not wearing boots any more. I asked to be allowed to wear shoes but was told only officers can do that.'

The next letter stated: 'I'm finished with the army. Either I'm going to spend the rest of the war in hospital or I'm going to become an officer.' He was accepted for OCTU and started his training jumping over ditches and ravines and living a rough life which he told me, 'is only worth it because there is an end in sight.' Flat feet weren't mentioned again. He succeeded in becoming an officer and did very useful service as an interpreter in the army of occupation.

* * *

It is summer 1945. British troops enter Berlin, Hans amongst them. Are Mutti and Onkel Franz alive? We hadn't heard from them since the house-to-house fighting when the Red Army entered the city, and they hadn't heard from us. The front of Niebuhrstrasse 58 is burnt out but the back where Mutti lived is still standing.

Hans appears at the door. Onkel Franz looks through the peephole. 'A British soldier. I wonder what he wants.'

'Open the door.' Mutti says. 'Good God! Hans!' It is too much for Mutti. She has an hysterical attack and it takes Hans and Onkel Franz some time to quieten her.

'There is somebody I want to introduce you to downstairs in my jeep,' Hans says.

'Who is it?'

'When I visited Belsen just after liberation I met a beautiful, intelligent Hungarian girl called Judith. She's 17 years old. She and I are together all the time.'

Mutti told me that her whole body went cold when she heard this. Later, Hans told Mutti that he had fallen in love with Judith and wanted to marry her. Mutti said to me: 'He has a wife and two children at home in England. It's terrible. But look at me. I divorced your father because I had fallen in love with Onkel Franz. I was married three times. What can I say to Hans?'

When Hans returned to London with Judith he asked Gretel for a divorce. But they could not agree on custody of the children. Eventually, he and Gretel were reconciled. Hans never saw Judith again.

Hans did his best to make things easier for Mutti and Onkel Franz. 'Why do you sit in the dark?'

'Our electricity ration has run out.'

'Didn't you know that as a Victim of Fascism you are allowed a double amount? Do you have your extra ration of gas?' My parents had been unaware of these extra benefits.

'Why don't you have a telephone?'

'Only businesses are allowed to have a phone.'

'But Victims of Fascism are exempt. I'll see to it that you're connected.'

* * *

The British army considered Hans a successful officer and offered him the post of staff captain, but he refused. He wanted to go back to his business career, as export manager of a firm concerned with international trade. When he was in his fifties his firm was taken over by a rival company and he lost his job. With a wife, two teenage children and a big mortgage he became frantic about getting another job. At last he got an interview as import manager of a business importing glassware from the Soviet Union. The interview went off alright until the final part which he reported to me:

'Our firm gives two weeks holiday per year.'

'I'm used to three weeks.'

'We're sorry but we can't give more.'

'I've never worked for less than three weeks.'

'You've heard our offer. You'd better think it over and give us a ring in the morning.'

The next day Hans phoned: 'I like the job but I'm not prepared to accept less than three weeks' holiday.'

'We'll ring you back.'

He was given the job. He explained to me: 'If they really want me they'll give it to me with three weeks. If they don't want me it doesn't matter what I say.'

He retired when he was 67. Then he decided to study for a degree. Birkbeck College recognized his Abitur of 48 years earlier and when he was 71 he was awarded a B.A. Honours in History.

When he was 84, Gretel fell very ill and Hans managed to nurse her back to health. However this exhausted him and he went on his own to Switzerland to recuperate, returning in good health. In the evening he went to bed and the next morning Gretel found him dead. He had had a heart attack and died in his sleep.

5   Onkel Franz

I remember Onkel Franz from my earliest days. He had been a comrade at arms of my father during the First World War and they had been friends ever since. We had picnics together in the Grunewald with Tante Tainka, his wife, and after Mutti divorced Vati he became a frequent visitor. As Mutti lived alone, his presence livened up the company considerably.

On one occasion when I was seven I said to them: 'Why don't you get married?'

A few days later Mutti said: 'You know, we thought over what you said. You're quite right. We will get married. Thank you for giving us such a good idea.'

However Tante Tainka said to Onkel Franz: 'No, I won't give you a divorce.' So Onkel Franz offered her alimony of 150 Marks per month and she agreed. This payment hung around Onkel Franz's neck for the rest of his life. Due to the depression there was also a general cut in wages, and we were always short of money. We couldn't afford coffee beans, and had barley coffee as a substitute. When Mutti's illness forced her to buy more expensive painkillers she said to me: 'Don't tell Onkel Franz that I've to buy all these medicines. It only depresses him.' What kept Onkel Franz going was the promise of promotion – until this was barred by the Nazis.

Onkel Franz was a Protestant and when he told his friends about the proposed marriage they advised him not to go ahead with it. They said that if the Nazis came to power it would be difficult for him if he had a Jewish wife. The year was 1930, three years before Hitler became Chancellor. But Onkel Franz was not to be deterred and, to my great delight, they married.

Onkel Franz was a man after my own heart. One day he came home with a piece of rock: 'This is granite,' he explained. 'Can you see it glistening?'

'I can,' I replied.

'Would you like a rock collection?'

'Yes, please.'

So we went out into the countryside at weekends to collect different types of rock. This was the beginning of my rock collection. Every day when he came home, I was waiting for him to give me a new idea.

When I visited Vati every Sunday, we went to the pictures, Circus Busch, the Planetarium or the Zoo. I enjoyed these places but Vati never explained anything to me. He was kind, even indulgent. Whenever I said 'Vati, can we do this?' or 'Can we go there?' he said 'Of course Peter, let's do it.' It was boring to ask him for any favour; I always knew his answer in advance. When I wanted something from Onkel Franz, I had to think ahead because he never agreed to my wishes immediately. He would ask, 'Why do you want to do this?' then he argued with me, 'Is this really necessary?' or 'Explain why you want to do it.' He either granted the request or explained why he turned me down. I had absolute faith in his judgement, whilst I had little confidence in Vati. I knew Vati meant well, but how I wished he would sometimes assert himself. He never did.

On 1 May 1934 there was a public holiday. The radio announced: 'Berliners, young and old, are marching to the Lustgarten. Joseph Goebbels and the Führer will address them.' However on that day Onkel Franz said: 'Let's cycle to the Grunewald. We can catch waterfleas for our aquarium.' We found a shallow stretch of water in a lake with a lot of waterplants and filled our jam jars with waterfleas. This was a real adventure, and we made many similar cycle trips.

For a short while, we moved to Hermsdorf, a northern Berlin suburb, where we had a small garden. Onkel Franz built a tiny pool where we kept terrapins and salamanders. Their main food was earthworms, and Onkel Franz told me to dig in the garden to find worms, otherwise the animals would die. I spent hours digging furiously for them. We also had an enclosure with two tortoises, and a fishtank with guppies and swordfish. They all bred, so we had a special breeding tank too. All my spare time was spent looking after these animals. It was paradise to me.

However Hermsdorf proved too isolated for us, so we moved back to a flat in Charlottenburg: Niebuhrstrasse 58.

'Peter, you've got to get rid of our terrapins, salamanders and tortoises,' said Onkel Franz, but seeing I was heartbroken, he added: 'Come, let's go to a pet shop. You can pick a parrot.'

We called it Lorchen. It was kept in my room and allowed to leave the cage. I trained it to be tame and to speak. Eventually it would sit on my shoulders babbling away, and I felt proud and happy.

* * *

Onkel Franz was marketing manager of WIBU, a co-operative supplying Catholic and Protestant institutions such as hospitals, monasteries and convents with household equipment. Twice a year he travelled throughout Germany demonstrating the latest refrigerators and washing machines. He was a keen photographer and took many films on each trip. On winter evenings at home he projected them on to a screen and told us about them.

'This is the Bamberg Cathedral. Can you see the little statues at the side? They are so comical.'

One day he said: 'You know, convents and monasteries are the only places where nobody discusses politics. They are not like the Protestant institutions which they try to Nazify. They don't want to antagonize the Catholic Church.' Onkel Franz found tranquillity among monks.

But at work he faced terrible challenges. He had been the editor of a house magazine, and was obliged to belong to a union. But the union excluded from membership Gentiles married to Jews. The director said: 'You can carry on editing the journal. But it will have to appear under my name.' Onkel Franz was due for promotion. He was told: 'Sorry, we can't consider you on account of your Jewish wife. But if you agree to a divorce you can go straight to the top.'

One Sunday night when I came home from a visit to Vati, Onkel Franz was sitting at the dining room table with his head in his hands. He had just stamped on his spectacles and smashed them. He was crying, whilst Mutti sat in a corner looking quite distraught. I was terrified.

After a long silence, Onkel Franz got up and said: 'Is it my fault that we have a government of criminals?'

The next day Mutti said to me: 'Go to Onkel Franz and ask him whether it might not be a good idea if we lived apart. This might help his work situation.' I was 13 years old and I knew very well that she was suggesting that he take advantage of the new Nazi laws on divorce. She used me as a go-between. I delivered the message, which was received in complete silence.

After a day or two, the cloud seemed to have lifted from the marriage. Onkel Franz had decided to stand by Mutti, come what may. Because of his decision he became more tranquil and life continued as normally as was possible. His stand saved Mutti's life: because she was married to a non-Jew she was not deported.

Onkel Franz continued to be subject to chicanery. In 1944 he was called up to a forced labour camp near Boulogne where he had to build the West Wall. The camp was guarded by Belgian and Italian fascists, and the inmates were all non-Jewish men married to Jewish wives. It was announced that anybody who agreed to divorce their wives would be released at once. Those who did found that their wives were immediately deported, but almost all refused.

The guards beat Onkel Franz with rifle butts. He collapsed and was taken to a field hospital with internal bleeding, and he lost his sight in one eye. He was released, a broken man, but he did not divorce Mutti.

Herr Witte, a family friend, also a Christian married to Mutti's best friend, was incarcerated in the same camp. He could not stand the treatment and committed suicide. The following week his wife was deported to Theresienstadt.

After the war the Berlin Senate classified Onkel Franz a 'Victim of Fascism' and he was given extra rations to recover. One day he received a phone call from the WIBU telling him that Herr Sendler, the managing director, had been dismissed because of his party membership, and the board had decided to offer the post to Onkel Franz. Finally his life's ambition seemed to have been fulfilled. But it was too late; his health would not allow him to accept the offer.

* * *

Onkel Franz developed stomach ulcers, and in 1946 the ulcers burst. He was rushed to St Hedwig's Hospital, which was run by Catholic nuns. A subsequent operation revealed cancer, which had already affected several organs. After his operation his pain eased, and this gave Onkel Franz the impression that he was on the road to recovery. The doctors did not want to shatter his belief.

He said to me one day: 'You know, this is a miracle. A sign of God towards the true faith.'

To us all – doctors, nuns, Mutti, and myself – he made much of his miraculous 'recovery' due to the mercy of God.

He said to the nuns who were his nurses: 'Please let me have a priest. I wish to convert to Catholicism.'

Two weeks before his death he was received into the Catholic Church. I had to be present at his baptism: I felt a participant in a ghastly scene of deception.

'I always wanted to survive Hitler,' he said, 'and I did.'

6   The Triumph of Love

In early 1943 Goebbels was looking for a present for the Führer's birthday on 20 April. He decided the perfect gift would be a Berlin free of Jews (*Judenrein*). Much of the work had already been done: in 1933 when Hitler came to power, 150,000 Jews lived in Berlin, by 1943 only 27,000 remained. Many had emigrated while others had been sent to camps. Of those left, most had been conscripted to work in war factories. Now Goebbels decided that the time had come for these Jews to be 'resettled' to the east.

The 27,000 Jews included 7,000 in mixed marriages. To compel Gentiles to divorce their spouses they were humiliated, as happened to Onkel Franz. Only seven per cent did divorce, and the minute they did, the Jewish spouse, suddenly unprotected, was sent to a camp. The 2,000 Jewish men married to Christian wives were working with their fellow Jews as forced labour. The date of 27 February was to be the last day of freedom for all remaining Berlin Jews.

Goebbels was anxious that the operation should succeed. Previously, when Jews had been given notice of evacuation, many had disappeared before the day arrived: this time secrecy was to prevail. Goering opened his air ministry as an assembly point, and Hitler gave permission for his Leibstandarte Adolf Hitler – his bodyguard troops – to be used for the mass arrest. The Jews were to be seized in the factories where they worked. As soon as the Jews arrived on the morning of that day, the Gestapo and the SS bundled them into lorries and then they were driven to collecting centres to await transport to Auschwitz. The 2,000 men married to Christians were taken to a special assembly point, the former Jewish community centre in Rosenstrasse.

* * *

In 1994 the BBC sent me to Berlin to make a film on Onkel Franz. They asked me to interview survivors of mixed marriages under the Nazis, and I spoke to Charlotte Israel, who was by then a frail woman of 85 in a wheelchair. This is her story.

* * *

'On 27 February 1943 my mother received an anonymous phone call: "Julius, your daughter's husband [who was Jewish] has been arrested." Mother and I went immediately to the police station in Grolmanstrasse. Here we were told: "Go to Rosenstrasse, the former Jewish welfare office, where you'll get more news." A kind policeman explained to us how to get there.

'When we arrived we found several hundred women whose Jewish husbands had been arrested and incarcerated in this building. We were refused entrance, but we knew the law and said to the Gestapo who were guarding the entrance: "By law it is illegal to refuse entry to a public building. You must let us in." This argument disconcerted the Gestapo, which tried to maintain a veneer of legality over its actions. They let us pass messages to our husbands but still refused to let anyone in.

'More and more women arrived, and by the following day something like 1,000 wives thronged the street. The few police present were overwhelmed. Traffic was diverted and bystanders swelled the crowd. The next day we were nearly double in numbers. I think we must have been at least 2,000 women, and this gave us courage.

'"*Gebt uns unsere Männer wieder!* – Give us our husbands back!" we cried. The authorities hoped the bitter winter nights would disperse us but we stayed.'

'How did you keep warm?'

'There was a café opposite. We took it in turn to get hot drinks.'

Goering's Air Force Day was on 1 March. To help the celebration, Britain's RAF launched the biggest raid yet on the capital: 1,000 people were killed, 6,000 were severely wounded and 7,000 houses were destroyed.

Charlotte continued: 'The building next to where the men were being held was hit. Thank God the prison was intact. We climbed on the ruins to glimpse our husbands through the windows.'

The previous week Goebbels had declared 'total war' as a result of the German surrender at Stalingrad. Three hundred thousand soldiers had been wiped out, and he ordered the mobilization of another one and a half million women. Hitherto German women had not been drafted into factories because in Nazi ideology a woman's place was in the home: they were not supposed to be interested in politics. Yet at Rosenstrasse 2,000 Aryan women were protesting against a fundamental aspect of government policy, and after six days they still refused to disperse.

Charlotte carried on with her story: 'The SS set up machine guns.

'"Murderers!" we women shouted. We were now oblivious to death threats. We felt that life without our loved ones was not worth living. I was thinking of Julius, who had a crippled leg, and how he must be suffering. The crowd now included soldiers in uniform on leave who were our brothers.

'One soldier shouted at the SS: "Cowards! We are fighting at the front, you want to shoot unarmed women!" One woman stood there in Nazi party uniform, wearing the gold badge of a long-term fighter for the Nazi Party. Her husband was the mayor of Potsdam and she was the sister of one of the protesters.

'I shouted loudest and was pushed to the front. An SS man called out, "Get back", but I took no notice.'

The SS hesitated – should they mow down these women? The Nazis were in a quandary and Goebbels recorded in his diary: 'The morale of Berliners is low.' The nearest overhead railway station, Börse, had to be closed because travellers could hear the women shouting. Goebbels wrote in his diary: 'The Gestapo reports some bystanders are sympathizing with the protesters.' The Nazis were always keen to claim that the population supported them in everything they did, and so far the deportation of Jews had been smooth.

But this protest was different: each Gentile wife had brothers, sisters, parents and friends, and if their partners disappeared everyone would know. Goebbels was told that shooting down 2,000 Aryans of the super-race would have repercussions. It would affect from 100,000 to 300,000 Germans. Mixed marriages also included many prominent artists. Goebbels made up his mind and ordered the men to be released – he would deal with them later.

Charlotte continued: 'I think it was on 6 March that the first dozen men appeared at the entrance of their prison. Their wives fell into their arms.

'"We're free," they shouted.

'"What happened?" we asked.

'"We don't know. They just said we could go home. No reason was given."

'A few minutes later another batch appeared. Julius was not released until the following day.'

* * *

But 25 husbands were still missing – they had been sent to Auschwitz before the release order came. The men's wives besieged the Gestapo headquarters at Burgstrasse. 'Goebbels has ordered the men's release. How can you act against his orders?' Their words struck a raw nerve. For generations it had been drilled into Prussian officialdom that obedience to orders was a matter of life and death. Then, the unbelievable happened. Berlin's Gestapo chief ordered that the 25 be returned to Berlin. At Auschwitz they had already been tattooed with numbers and been told what fate awaited them.

Germans knew of the existence of Auschwitz, but it was seen as a concentration not an extermination camp – the Nazis made sure the general population had no idea what was really going on inside. The 25 were brought back to Berlin only after signing statements that under pain of death they would not divulge what they had seen. They were given special training on how to reply to questions on Auschwitz:

'Were you beaten?'

'No, never.'

'That didn't sound convincing. Try again. Did you have enough to eat?'

'Oh yes. It wasn't marvellous but it was adequate.'

The prisoners had to practise giving satisfactory answers. Even so they could not be freed: they were sent to a work camp in Gross-Beeren, near Berlin, where their wives saw them daily. With the other 2,000 Jewish husbands of Christian wives, they survived the war.

Determined not to spoil Hitler's birthday treat, Goebbels announced: *'Berlin ist Judenrein.'* But what about the 2,000 Jewish husbands still wearing the Star of David badge walking the streets of Berlin? It was decided that they could stop wearing the badge.

* * *

In October 1995 the Berlin Senate and the Jewish community finally paid tribute to the women by creating a sculpture garden on the spot where their husbands were held. The sculptures, by Inge Hunzinger, stand in the grounds of the former Jewish welfare office in Rosenstrasse.

7   Caminchen, the House on the Hill

The year was 1929, and I was looking forward to the long summer holiday which was nearly upon us. I was six years old.

'Where am I going for the big holidays?'

'To Detta Emma in Caminchen.'

'Hurray! Who's taking me?'

'Vati.'

* * *

The train arrived at Lübben station. The saleswomen rushed to the platform carrying large trays. *'Saure Gurken! Saure Gurken!'* they shouted. These large cucumbers are pickled and eaten with your fingers; they are a speciality of the area. Every year Mutti sent me to Detta Emma's cottage during the long summer holidays. Her cottage was some distance from the village, on a hill. Her husband, Onkel Domke, now retired, had been a miller, and had owned a windmill built on the same hill. The mill burnt down many years before I began to visit, but we used to play in the ruins.

Caminchen had around 300 inhabitants at that time. It is in the Spreewald about 75 miles south-east of Berlin. Because the River Spree frequently overflowed its banks the land was marshy. The soil was poor and the peasants were often in debt.

The cottage was surrounded by a meadow full of wild flowers – dandelions, cowslips, daisies, cornflowers, buttercups, forget-me-nots, wild pansies. The grass grew so high that we could play hide-and-seek in it. At times I exclaimed, 'An egg!' if a chicken had laid an egg in the meadow instead of in the chicken run. All the children screamed with delight, pricked it and took turns to suck it dry.

* * *

'Peter, seven o'clock. Time to get up,' Detta Emma shouted. This wasn't really necessary because the chicken run was outside my window and I was woken up by a crowing cockerel. I got up and went to the pump for my morning wash. There was an outside toilet consisting of a seat over a bucket which Onkel Domke emptied daily and used for the vegetable garden

'Breakfast is ready.' I got a huge slice of black bread with linseed oil. Butter was not used in the village – 'we sell the butter to the town,' Detta Emma explained – but the bread and oil tasted good to me, a delicious change. Everything was new and thrilling, and I loved it.

After breakfast we sat on the veranda and peasants passed us on their way to their strips of field. 'Onkel Domke, why don't people have horses for drawing their carts?'

'People are too poor for that. Only the Pöhla family can afford horses. The rest have oxen. And the very poor ones use cows. I'm sorry for them.'

'Why are you sorry?'

'If you use cows for pulling they yield less milk.'

'Why are they so poor?'

'These people have only one strip of land. Here comes Pöhla. Morning.'

'Morning, Domke. Will it rain today?'

'Look at the clouds.'

'Yes, I know. Let's hope it'll be a short one.'

'Oh I'm sure it will. Anyway, in this heat the corn'll soon dry.'

'Hope so.'

'Peter, like to come with me?' I was waiting for an invitation and jumped on to the farm-cart to go to the field.

'Mr Pöhla, why don't you wear shoes?'

'Shoes are very expensive, Peter. We wear them only on Sundays. We're lucky. Some of the peasants don't even have Sunday shoes.'

'I wish I could go barefoot. My feet hurt.' By this time we had arrived.

'I'll get my scythe and start mowing. You walk behind me and do what Mrs Pöhla does.'

'Yes Peter, you can help us binding the corn into sheaves.'
'How do I do that?'
'Just watch us.' I enjoyed doing the work, and they were pleased to have an additional helping hand. 'The corn has to dry now,' the wife explained. An anxious day followed, with everyone praying for dry weather.

'It's dry now. Can you help us load the corn on to the wagons?' They really wanted my help. We took it to the barn for threshing. There was one threshing machine in the village and threshing was done in rotation. Ploughing followed.

'There isn't much for you to do now.' But it was enough for me to walk behind Pöhla when he ploughed.

* * *

One morning I went to the Pöhlas and found them in great agitation. I thought a member of the family had been taken ill. No, it was a horse.

'Yosser has broken his leg.'
'When a horse breaks its leg, it doesn't heal.'
'What are you going to do?'
'We're waiting for the knacker to fetch him.' As Mr Pöhla said this a howl came from the rest of the family. Yosser was neighing and so were the other horses. 'They all know what will happen to Yosser,' Pöhla explained. I was amazed at the bond between animals and people on the farm.

Childhood Paradise

In the evenings during the long summer Detta Emma and Onkel Domke read the paper by the light of a paraffin lamp. We children gathered under the heavy branches of a huge cherry tree outside Onkel Domke's cottage to chat or play games. These were the happiest times I ever knew in Germany. During the war I dreamt again and again of us children playing under the cherry tree.

Some days I went with the children to a nearby pond to swim. Or we gathered bilberries in the forest. Often Onkel Domke said: 'Peter, let's go for a walk with Lappack.' This was his dog, a large yellow mongrel who was my constant companion. When Lappack found a rabbit warren he burrowed furiously as he scented the rabbits. He was too big to get into the tunnels but he became so excited at the thought of catching a rabbit.

I loved exploring the farmyard. Until I stayed at Caminchen I had never seen anything like this. I saw how the cockerel watched over the cackling chickens. I looked at the goat tied to its post, struggling to get hold of a blade of grass just outside its reach.

The pigs and piglets fascinated me most. I witnessed the slaughtering of a pig – I'll never forget the horror of the scene. The butcher hammered an axe on the squealing pig's head until it passed out. Everybody looked on approvingly and the cruelty affected no one. A vein was cut and the blood collected in a vessel. A fire had been lit in the yard and the blood was made into black pudding which was handed round to be consumed. This was part of the feast of slaughtering a pig.

Occasionally we cycled to Neuzauche, which had a post office, a railway station and a bus stop. Caminchen had none of these, and was half a mile from the nearest made up road. There were only mud tracks which became impassable when it rained. Vati visited us at weekends. He was treated with respect by all the farmers. As a city man he knew what was going on in the world. People greeted him with: 'What's new in Berlin?' and he had to give an account of the latest happenings. It was not long before Nazism reared its head in Caminchen.

The Nazis expounded the slogan *Blut und Boden* – blood and soil. They believed in a mystical connection between those who tilled their own soil and the well-being of the nation. One day all peasants were called to a meeting. A Nazi official explained: 'The Führer knows how hard you work and yet you are in debt. Therefore, he has proposed the following: that the government is willing to take over your debt. The state will guarantee the price for everything you grow. As we want Germany to be self-sufficient in food there will be no difficulty in selling your produce. But if you run into debt again, the state will take over your farm. Think it over. If you agree, sign an agreement with us.'

As the peasants were poor they found the offer attractive and they signed up. In 1937 Detta Emma told Mutti: 'I'm sorry to have to tell you, there are some Nazis in this village who object to Jews coming here. I fear Peter will feel uncomfortable if he comes here again.'

That was the end of Caminchen. I had spent six happy summers there. During the war while Detta Emma was away on one of her nursing duties Onkel Domke disappeared on his way home after an evening visit to the Pöhlas. It was presumed he fell into one of the bogs, but his body was never found. Detta Emma died shortly after the war.

Return to Caminchen

Fifty years later I wanted to show my family my childhood paradise and we made our way by car to Caminchen. As we approached the village I wondered whether I could find my way to the House on the Hill. I had a clear image of where it was situated: from the centre of the village go straight ahead, take the first turning on the right and the house should become visible on the left on elevated ground. But would my memory play tricks? As we passed through the village the inhabitants gazed at the foreign car. It was still part of East Germany, being five years before the wall came down. They had never seen an English car before.

The road which used to be a mud track was now made up and used for exercises by the Red Army. I said to Sylvia: 'Now we should see the house.' Yes there it was! It looked just as it had in my imagination – only the veranda used to be open and now it was glazed. I stopped the car where the mill ruins had been and where we used to play hide-and-seek. The ruins were no more and the cherry tree had gone.

I rang the bell, and a man appeared. He looked at us and then at the car with English number plates.

'Is your name Domke?'

'Yes.' He was surprised. I was elated that a Domke was still living there.

'I don't know how old you are, but if you are about 60, you played with me as a child.'

He looked at me in amazement. He could not make out what I wanted. 'I'm 51,' he said.

'You must have been a baby when I played with your

sisters.' He seemed to think hard. I had not told him my name.

'Are you Peter from England?' He had heard his family speak of me.

We celebrated in the village pub and we soon found out how unpopular the communists were.

'Do you see the barley growing outside?' He pointed to a huge barley field. 'This morning's paper announced that the entire barley harvest has been gathered in our region. Those are the lies they're telling.' Everybody in the pub agreed.

I then went to Pöhlas' farm. A young girl answered and I explained myself briefly. She called her parents. Herr Pöhla was also too young to have known me. Then he suddenly asked: 'Are you Peter from England?' He fetched a bottle of Sekt. 'The communists are terrible.' he said. He checked himself as his daughter re-entered. When she left he continued. 'You have to be careful what you say in front of her. She's in the Party. Erna, my older sister with whom you played, is celebrating her birthday in the next village. Let's give her a surprise and go there.'

Erna lived with her daughter in a large farmhouse with stables which had an even larger garden full of fruit trees – peaches, apricots, red and blackcurrants and raspberries. There were about 20 people present.

'Peter from England. Welcome!' Several remembered me.

'Have some strawberry cake.'

'That's my favourite. It's July and I didn't see any strawberries in the market. How is it you have them?'

'We grow them on our private plot. If we sold them in the market we'd get nothing because of price control, so we eat them ourselves. Have some whipped cream – you won't get this in the shops either.'

We munched the delicious cake.

'The government is awful.'

'It can't be too bad. You're all wearing shoes now. You didn't when I was here last.'

'I know we're better off. We can even go on holidays now, something we couldn't have dreamt of before. But that's not the point – it's collectivization. They've taken away our land. *Honecker ist ein Räuber!* – Honecker [the President] is a robber!'

Robert, Erna's son-in-law, a plumber, added: 'You know,

we're working on materials which we know are no good. We complain, but nothing is done.'

But most of the conversation centred on old times: who had died, who was still around, what happened to each of us during the last 50 years and what we were doing now.

I felt both sad and pleased when we finally left the village. Caminchen had meant the happy past to me. For a moment I had glimpsed my childhood.

8   Education for Death

Endless columns were marching along the street. The Kurfürstendamm was a broad thoroughfare and the dense crowd stretched as far as the eye could see. There were Brown Shirts and Blackshirts and swastikas everywhere. The leader shouted 'Germany' and the crowd answered, 'Awake!' Then the leader shouted 'Jews!' and the answer came back, 'Perish!'

I shuddered and looked around to see whether anybody recognized me. A woman next to me exclaimed under her breath: 'Germany awake, Hitler perish.' I seemed to be the only one who had overheard her and I looked at her sympathetically. I told my mother about that woman and she said: 'She must be a communist.'

I was nine years of age, and it was 1932. The times in Berlin were exciting. There was nothing routine any more. There were marches, strikes, talk of revolution – everybody felt that something was going to happen. Boredom made me wish for excitement but anti-Semitism made me apprehensive.

Then it happened. On 30 January 1933, Hitler became Chancellor. What would become of us? His first object was to eliminate his political opponents: communists, socialists and liberals. Then on 1 April he started on us Jews: civil servants and teachers were dismissed, doctors and lawyers were not allowed to practise, Jewish businesses were boycotted, Jewish children were banned from grammar schools. But we still had friends in some quarters.

On 4 April President Hindenburg wrote to Hitler: 'I have been told that Jews have been dismissed from their post, even though they had served in the army during the last war. In my opinion people who have risked their lives for the Fatherland should continue in their profession.'

Hitler was not yet sufficiently secure to oppose the President. The following day Hitler replied: 'I believe our regulations are justified but I have acceded to your request and new orders will be issued.'

'You see, he can't do what he likes,' my father said. As most Jews had fought during the war they were re-instated. This gave us a false sense of security. Instead of packing our bags and fleeing we stayed put, until for many of us it was too late.

* * *

'Peter, you can go to your new school. *Ich war Frontkämpfer* – I fought in the front line.'

I was ten years old and about to enter the Grunewald Gymnasium, a selective grammar school in Berlin. Then it was announced on the radio: 'The government has decided to extend the Easter holidays for one month.' I couldn't believe my ears. Was this true? I had to find out so I cycled to the school. Yes it was true. With the stroke of a pen German schoolchildren throughout the country became Nazi supporters.

The extra month was not wasted by the authorities. A new headmaster, a Party member, was chosen for every school and 'unreliable' teachers were dismissed. At my school, the Grunewald Gymnasium, Dr Waldvogel was appointed.

Nazification of the school started right at the outset. At the beginning and end of every lesson we had to stand, raise our right arm and shout '*Heil Hitler*'. I was in a quandary. How could I greet Hitler? If I didn't it would be breaking the rules. I decided to compromise, so I raised my arm but I didn't shout '*Heil Hitler*'.

One day in the first term there was an announcement that there would be no lessons today; instead the entire school would visit the local cinema for a film. We were all delighted. The film was called *Hitlerjunge Quex*, with the well-known actor Heinrich George. It was a story of a communist father and his son, and how they were both converted to Nazism. Heinrich George had been a communist himself in real life, and in this film he rehabilitated himself in the eyes of the Nazis. 'A smashing film!' my classmates thought.

I envied those who joined the Hitler Youth, went on weekend hikes and attended weekly group evenings. I thought they were so lucky. They didn't have to do any homework when they were busy with the H.J. (Hitler Youth). But I had to sit at home and work hard.

Some teachers used every opportunity to tell us thrilling stories from the war: 'Modern war is a war of machines,' they said. 'Tanks and planes have taken over from hand-to-hand fighting.' We loved to hear these stories; they were a relief from ordinary lessons. During school outings to the countryside we were encouraged to play war games (*Geländespiele*) – a hunting party sets out to catch another party which was hiding. War was fun and if ever we had to fight it would be exciting.

One day our class teacher said: 'I'm going to tell you something I'm not really supposed to divulge.' We pricked up our ears. He lowered his voice confidentially: 'Tomorrow afternoon at the launching ceremony of the Labour Corps Headquarter the Führer will appear. It will be the first time he has visited our district.' A murmur of wonder went through the class and the boys arranged a meeting place to greet the Führer. But I had to stay at home. It was inevitable that I felt left out, and I wished secretly I could join in the fun and excitement – I wished I belonged to the superior Aryan race.

Some teachers appeared in the uniform of stormtroopers and a few made anti-Semitic remarks. Our Physical Education (PE) teacher Herr Neumann, made the entire class do punishment PE drills because 'one of the Jew-boys didn't pay attention'. Our music teacher, who always dressed in Nazi uniform, taught us Nazi songs, one of which had the refrain: '*Wenn's Judenblut vom Messer spritzt, dann geht's nochmal so gut* – When Jewish blood gushes forth from your knife, you can work much better.' The teacher told us Jewish boys that we didn't have to join in the refrain as it might upset us. (Unsurprisingly 50 years later, at a class reunion, not a single classmate could remember the singing of that song.)

The Nazis wanted good soldiers and laid much emphasis on PE. It was a main subject and we had P.E. lessons every day. I was overweight and hopeless at apparatus work like parallel and horizontal bars. I could not reach a satisfactory standard, and this made me anxious. I especially hated the horizontal bar. I couldn't raise myself; I hung from it like a sack of potatoes. Mutti made me join a Jewish sports club to improve my performance but it didn't make the slightest bit of difference.

The curriculum also included a new subject – National Politics. One of its topics was called Racial Theory. It was taught by the Professor of Biology. He was of medium height and had a beard. He had been on an Arctic expedition which had earned him the title of Professor: He explained: 'The world is divided into a number of races which can be distinguished according to the shape of their skulls. The highest development occurs in the Germanic longheads, the Aryans. 'Will the Jewish children stand up?' There were three of us. 'Prager come to the front.' I still remember my feelings while I stood there as the teacher measured my head. At first I was terribly frightened, but soon gathered courage when the teacher patted me on the back and said: 'There is no need to be afraid. I shall do you no harm. After all, it is not your fault that you are inferior.' Then he turned to the class. 'You see his skull is several centimetres shorter than this one,' and he pointed to a picture of Hindenburg on the wall. This kind of lesson not only gave the majority a sense of superiority but I no longer felt it strange when I was excluded from participating in playground games 'because I was a Jew.'

On one occasion my feeling of inferiority temporarily vanished. We were playing in the playground during break and one boy called out: 'Stupid Prager!' I don't know what overcame me, but suddenly I hit him. To my surprise, the other boys didn't take my opponent's part but instead, formed a circle to let us fight it out. To my further surprise the other boy was not stronger, as I had expected, but was actually frightened. Soon he had a bloody nose and was on the ground, while I, having lost my temper, continued to hit him. The circle of spectators attracted the teacher on duty who separated us and boxed my ears to punish and shame me. Far from shame, I felt elation. The other boys looked on at me with astonishment: the little Jew-boy had hit back and vanquished his Aryan opponent! It didn't seem to make sense. Just for one short moment I had lost my submissiveness and had asserted myself, but it couldn't last.

Segei Nagi was the son of the commercial attaché of the Japanese embassy. One morning he entered the classroom and said: 'On my way to school I saw the latest edition of *der Sturmer* in the showcase at Bismarck Platz. The way the Jews were shown and what they wrote about them was really disgusting. It's shameful.'

I pricked up my ears. Most of my fellow pupils went past this showcase and never commented. Perhaps I could be friends with him, ask him home and he wouldn't refuse like the others.

'Segei, would you like to come to my flat one afternoon and play soldiers? I have one hundred Germans and also a machine gun.' (Soldiers was the usual game played by German schoolchildren.)

'I'd love to. When?'

'Tuesday.'

'O.K. What's your address?'

'58 Niebuhrstrasse. Go through the main entrance, cross the back yard and we're on the third floor of the rear building. No lift.'

'You live across a back yard and then you've to climb three flights of stairs in a rear building?'

'That's right.'

'I'm sorry. I can't visit anybody who lives across a yard. My parents would never allow it.'

That was the end of my friendship with Segei.

* * *

Fifty years later I wrote to Segei Nagi's Tokyo home, thinking that we might renew our friendship.

He replied: 'I'm pleased you survived the war. We Japanese have never believed in racism. I must tell you about our rotten government. I own a block of flats in the centre of Tokyo. Of course it requires a lot of maintenance. Believe it or not our government taxes landlords to the hilt so that I make hardly any profit. How am I supposed to pay for the repairs? It is disgraceful and disgusting. I cannot tell you how the government infuriates me. What are property taxes like in your country?'

I did not write back.

* * *

In 1934 my parents moved to Hermsdorf, a northern suburb, and I went to the Hermsdorfer Realgymnasium. On my first day I was called to the headmaster's office. Only the headmaster, Herr Schulz, and my form teacher, Herr Henneck, were present.

'You are the only Jewish boy in the school. Only I and Herr Henneck know this. In my school nobody will be discriminated against because of their religion. I intend to keep it that way. You must promise not to tell anybody that you are Jewish. If for any reasons people call you names or show aggressive behaviour towards you, you must tell me immediately. I will not tolerate it. Do you understand?' Would that Dr Waldvogel of the Grunewald Gymnasium had behaved like this!

We had regular swimming lessons. Before we entered the water we had to take off our swimsuits and shower, and the first occasion we were asked to do this we felt terribly shy. We were in the first stages of puberty, and had never been nude among our classmates.

Our P. E. teacher noticed our embarrassment, and said: 'Come on, don't be silly.' To encourage us, he took off his trunks and showered, and we reluctantly followed suit.

I was the only Jewish boy and the only one to be circumcised. As soon as the others noticed this they all looked at me, while I looked at them in astonishment. The class started to whisper among themselves, pointing at me, whilst my embarrassment turned into horror. Finally several boys came to me, pointed to my penis and asked why mine was different from theirs. I was completely baffled and just said I'd ask my parents. However I felt too shy to consult them about such an intimate matter. My parents, like so many of their generation, were embarrassed about anything concerning sex. They could not name the sexual organ, and did not even explain about the Jewish ritual of circumcision.

* * *

My parents felt isolated in Hermsdorf and after a year we moved back to Charlottenburg. I therefore returned to the Grunewald Gymnasium.

During one of our German lessons, Dr Bart, our class teacher explained: 'Great men like Jesus Christ and Martin Luther only rarely appear on the earth but we are very fortunate because two great men live in our time – Adolf Hitler and Benito Mussolini.' On another occasion we had to take down the number of criminal offences committed by Jews and by Germans showing that Jews commit more crimes. The teacher said: 'You see, more Jews than Aryans are criminals. That's why we must exclude them from all public life. Learn the figures. You'll have a test on this.' When I told my mother, I saw the horror on her face and she said: 'You won't do this test. You will not go to this school any more. I'll find a Jewish school for you.'

Vati contacted the Goldschmidtschule and said to the head: 'I should like my son to go to your school but I can't afford the fees. What can I do?' Frau Dr Goldschmidt answered: 'Peter can start tomorrow. Don't worry about the money. I shall never refuse a child because of financial reasons. Just pay as much as you can afford.' Thus my days started at the Judische Privatschule Dr Leonore Goldschmidt.

9   Goldschmidtschule

My first day at school was overwhelming. 'How will I manage?' I thought. 'I've never been in a class with girls.' Twenty girls were staring at me as I was standing next to Herr Meissinger, the form teacher. He took my details. All the boys were seated on the left and the girls on the right.

'That's good,' I thought, feeling reassured, 'I'll sit with the boys.' Pupils were sitting in double desks. Herr Meissinger was surveying the scene. 'Prager, I can't see an unoccupied desk on the boys' side. You'll have to sit next to Inge Jaeger.' The seat next to her was the only empty one in the entire class. I was horrified. 'Oh dear, what am I to do?'

I walked towards Inge in a daze and sat down. She noticed my discomfiture. She smiled at me and pushed a piece of paper towards me, inviting me to play noughts and crosses. I hesitated. 'Now she wants me to play. If the teacher finds out, he'll be annoyed. I know she's trying to be nice. All right I'll play.'

A boy said to me: 'You know, every Nazi says, Jews are no good except the one they know personally – he is the exception. When you add up all the exceptions the figure will be bigger than the entire Jewish population.' We laughed. Many other jokes were told. At Pesach we dared each other to cross the Kurfürstendamm eating a piece of matzos.

I made friends and participated fully in the life of the school. I took part in the school play – A Midsummer Night's Dream – in which I played Thisbe. I felt relieved that no particular emphasis was laid on physical education. The school didn't intend to turn out soldiers.

I will never forget the pleasant feeling of being approved by my peers. Dr Leonore Goldschmidt succeeded in her aim of providing for her pupils a haven of peace in a hostile environment. However, my teachers didn't appreciate my feeling of elation. Having no more constraints my classroom behaviour deteriorated. In my school report of October 1938, my form teacher Fräulein Schlesinger wrote: 'His behaviour is somewhat childish and uneven.' She omitted this sentence in my leaving report, as she didn't want to spoil the start of my new life in England.

All the staff were sympathetic towards pupils except Dr Lewent. He was tall and thin and wore glasses. He never smiled. He was of the old school, and believed that the best way to make children learn was by fear. He would shout and scream and use sarcasm to maintain discipline. During my 40 years' experience as a teacher, I always had him in mind as an example of how not to teach. We had continuous written and oral assessment. Teachers assessed oral work by giving marks from 1 to 6 – 5 and 6 being fail marks. Dr Lewent's method was to ask a question and then call out a name. The person had to stand up and give an answer. If you didn't know, it was best to say something as you might guess correctly. If you said nothing, Dr Lewent shouted: 'Five, sit down!' On one occasion he asked me: 'When did Frederic the Great reign?' I didn't know, but to avoid a five I replied. 'Sometime in the eighteenth century.' To this Dr Lewent said: 'Prager, do you know what an ox is?' (In German somebody who is stupid is called an ox.) 'What am I to reply?' I asked myself. I started to panic, 'You must say something. You don't want to get a five.' I stood up and said: 'An ox is a female bull.' My answer was received in complete silence. Then a slight giggle went through the row of pupils. It stopped immediately when they saw Dr Lewent's furious eyes. I was completely overwrought by my own answer. I feared the worst. 'He'll give me five. He'll send me to the head.' We all watched Lewent's every movement. No doubt he thought, 'Prager is trying to poke fun at me. The rascal!' After a pause which seemed eternal he said, 'Sit down!' The lesson continued as though nothing had happened.

Our history teacher Dr Goldschmidt (the headmistress) told us: 'Disraeli was, as a child, ashamed of his Jewish hooked nose. He tried desperately to alter its shape by pushing up the end of his nose with his finger.' I thought as my own nose was slightly bent maybe I could do something to make me look more Aryan. Dr Goldschmidt's anecdote, meant to amuse us, inspired me to emulate Disraeli. Every night in bed I pushed up the end of my nose, hoping for the impossible. In the morning I looked in the mirror but could detect no alteration – I just would not look 'Germanic'. I did this nose pushing regularly until I came to England.

The Girls

Lore Pieck was dark and had brown eyes. She sat in the desk behind me. She spoke in a husky voice and always wore an enigmatic smile. I was infatuated with her. I gazed at her at breaktime, hoping nobody would notice as I was terribly shy. I cycled to school past her house. I desperately hoped she'd come out so that we could cycle together. Sometimes I was successful and sometimes not; I was much too diffident for an open approach. I was elated when I managed to be with her, but she had no interest in me. Other boys were more forward and more successful.

Another girl who took my fancy was Tutta Goldschmidt, the daughter of the headmistress. One day I was invited to the house of my friend Hans Goldmann. Tutta was there, and we played in the garden. In one game we had to give the girls piggy-back rides. Hans said: 'It's your turn to carry Tutta.' It was heavenly to carry such a blissful burden. However I was unable to tell her of my feelings and she never found out.

Stella Goldschlag was also a member of my class. She was strikingly pretty with beautiful fair hair – we called her the blonde bombshell. Not only the boys but the young male teachers seemed to make eyes at her. To me she was quite out of reach. One day Onkel Max took me to a performance organized by the Jüdische Kulturbund. As we were waiting for the curtain to rise my uncle suddenly got up and greeted none other but Stella whom he apparently knew. She was wearing a long, low-cut dress and he started to flirt with her, joking about her low cut back. I felt embarrassed by his behaviour, and wished he would stop. When I emigrated she faded from memory... Until 1992, when at a Jewish schools reunion in Berlin a former pupil who had survived underground in Berlin said 'Stella had been a 'greifer'. The

Gestapo employed her to catch Jews who were hiding from deportation. After liberation the Russians sent her to prison for ten years. She is still living in Germany.

* * *

Our school was an examination centre for the University of Cambridge and we were prepared for the Cambridge School Certificate. In addition to my German subjects my timetable contained English Arithmetic, English Geography, English History and Art. I had opted for Art, for which I had no talent, because my parents had told me to listen to English as much as possible. As these teachers spoke no German we learned English by the direct method. We tried to find out what the teachers thought of the Nazis but they would not discuss politics. We had the impression that they thought our school, being fee paying, was like an English public school... Until November 1938.

10   *The German Lesson*

It is 10 November 1938, and I cycle to school as usual. A large number of fire engines race along in all directions and I wonder why. However, my mind is concentrating on the German lesson, as this morning we have our monthly essay test. I don't like working under pressure but this test is important because my result will dictate whether I go up the following year. I'm only just satisfactory and Dr Lewent is a strict teacher. I wonder what we will have to write about.

However, as soon as I had arrived at school I noticed the general consternation of my classmates.

I asked: 'Why are there so many fire engines racing about? Where is the fire?'

'Don't you know? They set the synagogues alight!'

'Who did?'

'The stormtroopers, you idiot. The fire engines won't extinguish the flames but are preventing the neighbouring buildings from burning'.

Inge was crying: 'They took my father at six o'clock this morning. He's gone to Sachsenhausen Concentration Camp.'

It is eight o'clock and the school bell rings. We file into our classrooms and make ourselves ready for the test. Dr Lewent enters and says in a matter of fact voice: 'Due to special circumstances school will close after the first lesson. The test will take place and the title of the essay is on the blackboard.'

On the blackboard was written: 'Give your views on the significance of the failure of the Romans to defeat the Germanic tribes in the Teutoburger Forest.' I wonder how I shall manage it, but I start.

After only ten minutes Frau Dr Goldschmidt bursts into our classroom. 'Pens down!' she shouts. 'There's a mob outside the main entrance threatening to burn down our school. Leave everything and go out by the back!' Thank God I don't have to finish that wretched essay. But what will happen when I leave the building?

Scared, we hurry out of the building. The jeering Hitler Youth are playing truant and probably include my former classmates form the Grunewald Gymnasium. They don't realize that we are leaving by the back door. Meanwhile the caretaker, a Gentile, together with Philip Woolley, the Oxford graduate who taught us English, stood in front of the main gate armed with sticks warding off any approaching Hitler Youth.

* * *

That afternoon Dr Goldschmidt, the headmistress, summoned Mr. Woolley to her home. 'Mr Woolley,' she said to the astounded young teacher, 'I would like you to take over the school.'

Mr. Woolley thought he had not heard properly. 'What did you say?'

'I'll explain. The stormtroopers didn't burn down the 'Israel' Department Store along the Kurfürstendamm because the owner is a British subject. So our school might also be saved if I give it to you. Are you willing?'

Mr Woolley had to do some quick thinking. He was only 23, and has only recently left college. He had no teaching experience and could hardly speak German. How could he become the owner of a school in Berlin with over 500 pupils? But if he saved the school he'd be able to help the Jewish children to emigrate. 'Alright, I agree.'

'We thought you would,' said Mr Goldschmidt, the husband, who was a lawyer. 'I've prepared all the documents. They just need your signature.'

Mr Woolley signed. A short while later passers-by couldn't believe their eyes. The Union Jack was hoisted up the flagpole on the roof of the building. The school was not burnt down.

Three days later it re-opened. Several teachers were missing however; they had been arrested, and taken to Sachsenhausen concentration camp.

* * *

As I cycled home on 10 November, I first called to see how my father was getting on. On the way I saw crowds gathered around Jewish shops which had had their windows broken. I was frightened. I rang the bell of my father's flat and Tante Trude opened the door. She was crying.

'Vati has been arrested and taken to a concentration camp.'

While I commiserated with her there was a knock on the door. It was Frau Krause, the caretaker's wife. She was short and plump and when she spoke her face did not seem to convey the meaning of the words.

'I am so sorry about what has happened today,' she said. 'It's terrible isn't it?' After a minute or two she came to the point: 'With all these troubles, no doubt you don't wish to be lumbered with so many of your things. I just wanted to say, if there's anything you wish to get rid of: clothes, furniture, crockery, pictures or any valuables, my husband and I would be only too pleased to help you in disposing of them.'

In the afternoon my stepmother went to the army barracks to see Major Schmidt who had been a comrade in my father's regiment during the last war. He was on active service again and had kept in contact with my father in spite of the disapproval of the Nazis. He said he would do his best and write a letter to the commandant of Sachsenhausen on Paul's behalf. He did write a letter to the SS, but we shall never know whether it was due to his intervention that my father was eventually released.

Ten days after Vati's arrest we were called to a Jewish neighbour. 'I've just been freed and Paul has asked me to send you greetings. Don't worry, there's nothing to be afraid of. A concentration camp is just like an army camp, only you have SS guards on duty instead of soldiers.' We wanted to believe it.

When Vati was released after three weeks he said nothing about his treatment. 'I've had to sign a statement that I won't speak about the camp, otherwise I'll be re-arrested. Please don't ask me anything about what happened. I'm happy to be home.' From his behaviour I gathered that a concentration camp was nothing like an army camp.

Only a year later in England did Vati tell me about it. He suffered all the indignities which are so well known. But there was one occurrence which hit him particularly hard. During a cross-examination he was asked what he had done during the war.

He answered: 'I was a captain and won the Hanseatenkreuz for bravery.'

The interrogating SS man got up and slapped Vati's face. 'Liar!' he screamed. 'Jews are cowards. No Jew can ever win a medal for bravery.'

This event hurt Vati deeply: not the physical pain but the moral shock. This slap in the face finally killed his love for his country. He told me later, 'Anyone who says, "my country, right or wrong", has never been in a concentration camp.'

* * *

Hans Goldmann, the only Jew left in my old class at the Grunewald Gymnasium told me that the day after the pogrom one boy came to him and said: 'My parents and I want to express our deep regret for what has happened to the Jews.' It was the only remark made by a member of the class of 30 pupils. After the war I tried to find out who had said this. I contacted the Old Boys' Association but nobody could help me. During the war Hans visited my mother regularly. The last time he came was on 26 June 1942, my birthday. He looked haggard and Mutti gave him a plate of soup. He told her: 'My parents and my younger brother and sister have been deported. I'm lucky; I work for Siemens.' Then in 1943 the last transports were sent to Auschwitz and he no longer came to see my mother.

Leaving for England

Two days after the pogrom Mutti wrote a letter to my brother Hans in London. 'It isn't safe for Peter to remain here. Please do everything in your power to get him to England.'

A few days after the pogrom the Home Office announced that the government had decided to issue 10,000 visas to children from Germany immediately. Lord Baldwin opened a fund for bringing the children to Britain. My father bought *The London Times* regularly and every day we saw the names of subscribers to the fund, some giving only a few pence. I cried when I saw this: while the German people abandoned us, the British, most of whom had no connection with us, were giving money to help us. I felt grateful to Britain and a deep hatred towards the country of my birth.

Every day when I cycled to school I passed newly constructed army barracks along the Hohenzollerndamm. As I looked at these forbidding buildings I imagined myself placing bombs at the entrance and blowing them up. Berlin became more and more militarized. Soldiers in uniform were everywhere and army convoys would race through the streets, bringing all traffic to a halt as they had priority like emergency vehicles. When I saw these vehicles speeding along I wished I could stand somewhere with a machine gun and mow them all down.

Within two weeks my brother wrote: 'I've found a family for Peter. Mrs and Mr Flateau of Ilford, Essex, are willing to take him into their home. They want him to celebrate Christmas with them.'

'Hurray,' I shouted. I withdrew my savings of 100 Marks from the post office.

The official, a kindly man, asked: 'And what are you going to do with all this money?'

I said, proudly: 'I'm going to buy an English dictionary because I'm emigrating to England.' The man looked pleased and wished me good luck.

At the last minute the departure was postponed until after Christmas because the authorities had not prepared the papers in time. I was disappointed, but Mutti suddenly embraced me and started to sob. 'I'm so happy you're staying over Christmas,' she said. I was surprised at this because I thought that she would be sorry about the postponement. 'Don't you know how sad I am that you're going to leave me?'

'No, not really. Didn't you want me to go to England?'

'Yes, of course, we all do, but I still don't want to lose you.' I didn't understand this logic and was disconcerted by her outburst, but it didn't prevent me from looking forward to coming to England. I was going to a bright future. For years I had been looking forward to this, and nothing was going to stop my joy at starting a new life.

We left on 28 December via Hamburg. Mutti and Onkel

Franz were crying as I left, but Vati, who took me to the station, was really happy. I remember him waving furiously as the train was leaving the station. It was his concentration camp experience which made him happy I was going.

We were 44 children. I was one of the oldest, the youngest was two. The two year old was crying and was carried by one of the adults accompanying us – parents were not given visas. Some of the older boys had shaved heads, as they had just been released from a concentration camp. Outside our carriage stood two men who kept glancing at us. They had fierce looking expressions on their faces and appeared to be far from friendly. 'They must be Gestapo men,' we whispered to each other and remained silent for the rest of the journey.

I looked out of the window. It was snowing. Telephone wires raced past us. I saw trees and meadows passing. There was a country lane with farmhouses, and filling the lane was a column of army vehicles winding its way along slowly. All of us knew that war was coming; Hitler was not arming for peace.

'Surely Germany will be defeated,' I thought, 'because the whole world will be against her. Evil always loses in the end. One day I'll return to Germany but only as a soldier with an invading army.'

In the evening we boarded a ship of the United States Lines bound for Southampton. We left at high tide and two hours later we were outside territorial waters. We were free.

11 Domprobst Lichtenberg

'Isn't it stupid to be proud of being a Jew? I'm not proud of being persecuted.' My mother made this remark frequently. When she married Onkel Franz, our home became almost completely a Christian home. With the Nazis in power, my mother held the belief that a change of religion might make things easier for Onkel Franz. He had just been told that his promotion had been barred because he was married to a Jewess. However, the Nazi racial theory was not concerned with religion. To Nazis a baptized Jew was a non-Aryan and was treated just like a Jew.

Nevertheless, the Nazis strongly objected to Jews converting to Christianity. They succeeded in preventing the conversion of Jews by Protestant pastors, but the Catholic Church was less amenable to Nazi pressure. One outstanding anti-Nazi priest was Domprobst Lichtenberg who conducted conversion classes every Friday afternoon at St Hedwigskirche, Unter den Linden. My mother was one of his pupils, and he had great influence over her. After the class the pupils attended a public service at his church. It was always packed to capacity. The services regularly ended with the prayer: 'Let us pray for the priests in concentration camps, for the persecuted non-Aryan Christians, and for the Jews'. Then he turned to a prayer for the government: 'And they also will have to sit at the table with Abraham, Isaac and Jacob, and those who don't like it will have to remain outside.' Sometimes the black uniforms of the SS mingled in the congregation: on other occasions the seats nearest the pulpit were occupied by the Gestapo, who though in plain clothes, could usually be recognized by their demeanour. Lichtenberg started his sermon: 'I give a special welcome to the members of the SS and the Gestapo. I hope you come to the House of God in the spirit of repentance.'

On 10 November 1938 the church was so crowded that people were standing in the aisles. They waited for an uplifting sermon and were not disappointed: 'What was yesterday we know, what will be tomorrow we don't know, but what happens today we have witnessed ourselves. Outside the temple burns, the temple which is also a House of God. Those who destroy Houses of God are evil men. They should be treated the same way as if they had set alight a Catholic Church.'

It is difficult now to envisage how uplifting such words were when my mother recounted this to us at home, surrounded as we were by terrible gloom. How long could this man remain a free man? The Nazis were wary of attacking the Catholic Church because of its international power. In 1941 they started their euthanasia programme, in which hundreds of thousands of disabled people were killed without their relatives' consent. The programme was conducted by Dr Conti, the chief Nazi doctor. On 28 August 1941 Lichtenberg wrote to Dr Conti pointing out that euthanasia was murder under German law. This was too much for the Nazis and they awaited an opportunity to arrest him.

In October 1941 deportations of Jews to Auschwitz began. Goebbels distributed a leaflet countrywide dubbing any German who showed sympathy towards Jews a traitor. Lichtenberg wrote a sermon to be read the following Sunday at his church, wherein he called this pamphlet un-Christian, reminding his congregation of Jesus' command, 'Thou shalt love thy neighbour as thyself'. He was not to deliver the sermon. A Nazi Youth girl who strayed into his church to admire the architecture overheard one of his anti-Nazi sermons and went to the police to denounce him. He was immediately arrested. The Nazis had not been able to try him for his letter to Dr Conti because euthanasia was indeed unlawful. He was tried under the law against 'malicious gossip' (Heimtückegesetz). The prosecution was offered as evidence his various prayers for the Jews and also his unpublished sermon attacking Goebbels' leaflet. He was given two years imprisonment.

Towards the end of his prison term Lichtenberg expressed the wish that on his release he should be sent for pastoral duties among the Jews in the ghetto of Lodz, and permission was granted. But on the day of his release from Tegel prison he was re-arrested and sent to Dachau. He died on the way. The authorities allowed his body to be taken to Berlin for burial. A crowd of thousands followed his coffin, a silent anti-Nazi demonstration, the only one possible in those days. In 1997 on his visit to Berlin, the Pope beatified him.

Before his arrest Lichtenberg had baptized my mother. After the war she said to me: 'At the time I thought that I had real faith in Catholicism. I realize now it was not faith in the Catholic creed but faith in this remarkable man which had made me change my religion. I regret it now.'

I can think of no better epitaph for this good man than the quotation from Shakespeare's *Julius Caesar*:

'His life was gentle, and the elements
so mix'd in him that Nature might stand up
and say to all the world, "This was a man!"'

12   England

It is 31 December 1938. We dock in Southampton. Snow covers the countryside as the train takes us to Waterloo. I can see the tall figure of my brother Hans at the end of the platform. I race towards him. We embrace.

'How are things at home?'

'Vati has been released from Sachsenhausen. Onkel Franz is O.K. Mutti was crying when I left.'

We cross Waterloo Bridge. I'm here! I've arrived! Do wishes come true? They do! The red buses, all the signs in English, cars on the wrong side of the road, traffic jams, the policemen with their peculiar helmets, the huge advertising posters – I want to shout for joy. Hans is talking non-stop, 'Furniture to England', 'Home Office', 'Visa', 'Work permit', they're all odd words I can't make out. I'm in a trance, I've made it, I've made it!

Hans pulls me by the arm. 'Look out! If you keep looking the wrong way you'll be run over.'

I hear his voice but I'm dreaming. We board a bus. London traffic... people rushing about... everybody busy. The way to heaven must feel just like this.

We arrive at Hans' flat, Ashford Court, Cricklewood, a two-room apartment with a tiny kitchen. It's New Year's Eve. We phone Mutti and tell her that everything is alright.

* * *

The next day Hans took me to Mr and Mrs Flateau in Ilford. They had guaranteed the Home Office that they'd look after me. Sydney Flateau was of medium height, slim, slightly bald with a straight nose; Mary Flateau was short, thickset with black hair and a hooknose. To me they were rich. They owned a factory in the City where they made evening gowns with 50 employees. They had a car. They lived in a big house with a live-in servant. At weekends we went to their caravan in Roydon, Hertfordshire. They were communists and they wanted to help a victim of fascism – that's why I was there.

One of the first things they said to me was: 'Peter, we are Jewish but we don't keep a kosher house.'

'We didn't in Berlin either,' I answered, to their great relief.

'You know, we don't believe in religion,' they added.

'Nor do I,' I replied. This broke the ice and they were happy.

Mr Flateau said: 'I must tell you how Mary and I met. We didn't like the strictly Orthodox background of our parents. We wanted to break away. So quite independently of each other we joined an English cycling club, wanting to mix with English people and marry out. Well, we found each other!'

* * *

English food was terrible; it was starchy and the many different puddings and pies bound up my insides. In Berlin we never drank tea but here coffee was just about unknown, except for a liquid called Camp Coffee which seemed to have very little connection with coffee beans.

In Berlin I had been talkative but because I was not fluent in English I was unable to join in any conversation. One conversation I had with Mr Flateau did not go down at all well. One day I said that Hitler had done a good job in stopping unemployment. He just stared at me, horrified. But I continued and said if it weren't for the Nazis then Germany would be under communist rule and that would have been even worse. Mr Flateau retorted that I had been influenced by Nazi propaganda. I resented this at the time, but of course he was right. I had only read German newspapers which all carried Nazi propaganda. Inevitably I had absorbed Nazi ideas.

Once a week I visited Hans where I made up for the lack of conversation, talking German continuously from the moment I arrived until the moment I left.

The first letter from Mutti arrived: 'Don't forget to change your underwear regularly, and your pyjamas. Do you eat enough? What happens If you fall ill? Onkel Jean is not there.' He was our doctor. As I read the letter I rushed to my room and burst into tears. From then on every time I received a letter from home I started to cry.

* * *

'What do you want to be?' Mr Flateau asked.

'My parents want me to become a motor engineer.'

'All right, I'll fix you up a school where you can study the subject.' Thus I started at the Regent Street Polytechnic. In those days secondary education was not free and the Flateaus paid my fees.

15 January 1939. My first day at the Polytechnic. 12 o'clock. I go for lunch to the Lyons Teashop at the corner of Mortimer and Regent Street. I sit down and look at the menu. I have nine pence to spend. 'Tomato soup costs two pence, shepherd's pie is sixpence; that leaves one penny for a sweet. But all the sweets cost two pence! Ah, there is one for one penny – Yorkshire pudding.' A waitress appears. She is young and pretty and wearing an apron like all Lyons' waitresses.

'What would you like, sir?'

'Tomato soup, shepherd's pie, Yorkshire pudding.'

'Pardon, sir?'

'Tomato soup, shepherd's pie, Yorkshire pudding.'

'But Sir, Yorkshire pudding does not go with shepherd's pie.'

I am getting annoyed. 'I want Yorkshire Pudding!'

The waitress shakes her head and walks off. In German the word 'pudding' implies a sweet dish.

The waitress arrives with the soup. After the soup she brings the shepherd's pie. With it on a plate is a peculiar-looking crust. It isn't particularly nice but I'm hungry so I eat it. Then I wait for my pudding but the waitress arrives with the bill. 'Here you are, Sir.'

'Where is my Yorkshire pudding?'

'You've had it.'

'No I haven't.'

She points to the empty plate where the crust had been. I looked at her and the empty plate in disbelief. 'I told you, sir, that Yorkshire pudding does not go with shepherd's pie.'

I shrug my shoulders and look at the bill which includes the penny for the Yorkshire pudding. I pay and leave, thinking the English have odd eating habits.

* * *

A friend said: 'You know, an Austrian refugee chef has introduced real Viennese coffee to the Tottenham Court Road Lyons Corner House. They even sell continental cakes and there are newspapers on wooden frames.'

'Let's go!'

The Corner House became a haven for German and Austrian refugees – even the waiters were fellow refugees. If you went there at the weekend, you were bound to meet someone you knew.

At school I wore plus fours, specially bought by my mother to make me look English. I could always recognize my fellow refugees by their plus fours, as no English boy wore them. I don't know where German Jews got the idea of the typical Englishman's clothes. I felt so self-conscious wearing them that at the first opportunity I asked Mr Flateau to buy me something else to wear.

The end of term came, and with it my first school report.

I came eighth out of 23 in English. How could I be better than English boys? I was conversant with English grammar which English pupils found difficult. Academically I did well but in practical subjects, such as woodwork and metalwork, I came bottom – not a good start for a future motor engineer. Nevertheless I passed the entrance examination for the School of Engineering and left the Polytechnic in July 1939. After that I had no plans; the future was too uncertain.

* * *

Every weekend we went to the Flateaus' caravan in Roydon. It was situated along the banks of the River Lea where we could swim and boat. This was enjoyable, but nothing like the monthly visit to Mrs Flateau's sister at Hoses Farm, Essex. She was married to Leslie Plummer, the General Manager of Beaverbrook Press. Later he became a Labour MP and was knighted. Now I saw how the English upper class lived. Hoses

Farm was a large Tudor manor house surrounded by spacious grounds. They had a full-time gardener and two servants, and the luxury of the place put even Onkel Richard's villa in Werder to shame. The barn had been converted into a badminton court and the grounds included a tennis court, a large meadow, a vegetable garden and a small wood. We were woken by a servant bringing us tea and biscuits. Breakfast and all meals were taken in the dining area of the huge downstairs hall. There is a scene in the film of Bernard Shaw's *Major Barbara* where the rich Undershafts help themselves to a sumptuous breakfast served on silver platters. That scene reminded me of the breakfasts at Hoses Farm. All the meals were delicious. At lunch there were always two kinds of sweets: baked pies for the adults, jellies and custard for the children. I loved to eat the jellies and chocolate custard puddings but when Mrs Flateau said, 'Peter, have a pie!' I had to take one because I was an adult. Every afternoon new cakes were baked for tea.

* * *

Immediately after the invasion of Czechoslovakia, newspaper posters appeared in the streets of London: 'Germany demands the Polish Corridor!' and 'Poles suppress German minority!' An invasion of Poland was in the offing. At the same time another news item crept on to the hoardings: 'Gracie in hospital', 'Gracie Operation', 'Gracie latest', 'Gracie better'. Soon Gracie's health held a more prominent place in the news than the German threat to Poland. Who was this Gracie? I'd never heard of her. Was she the wife of a German general? or the wife of the Czech prime minister? Was 'Gracie Operation' a code-name for the mobilization of the British army? Perhaps she was a prominent politician arrested and tortured by the Nazis on their advance through Czechoslovakia. I didn't know, so I asked Mr Flateau: 'What is the connection between Gracie and Poland?'

He laughed. 'You obviously don't understand the English way of life. Gracie Field is a singer and her operation is much more important to the English than the Czech invasion by the Germans or the threat to Poland. Thousands of innocent people may be killed in concentration camps but the English are more interested in Gracie Field's health. That's the trouble with us. Because we're more concerned with such trivialities Hitler gets away with murder.'

I listened with amazement and just could not fathom the inscrutable mind of the English.

Vicky, the Hungarian-born cartoonist, recounted how in those days he saw a headline in the *Evening Standard*, 'England in Danger'. He rushed to buy the paper only to find out that the danger confronting England was being bowled out in cricket in Australia. The danger that England might be bowled out by Nazi Germany was never discussed.

13   Gracie's War

It is August Bank Holiday 1939 and the front page in the *Daily Express* carries the headline: 'There will be no War!'

On 1 September 1939, Germany invades Poland.

Mr Flateau says: 'War will break out. We'll take you to Hoses Farm. You'll stay there for the time being.'

On 3 September we listen on the radio to Chamberlain's ultimatum, and Mr Flateau comments: 'He should have been this firm at Munich.' Then turning to me: 'I wonder what your parents are thinking at this moment.'

'They'll be pleased.' I felt elated.

'Why?'

'Because this is the beginning of the end for the Nazis.' The phone rings

'For you,' says Mrs Flateau.

'Hello, Peter, it's me, Vati. I've just arrived.'

'How did you get here?'

'Well, as soon as they signed the Soviet–German Pact, I went to the British Embassy. I showed them my Home Office permit and they gave me a visa. I went to Friedrich Strasse station and bought a ticket and here I am. I caught the last train leaving Berlin for London.'

'You were lucky.'

'Yes. I'm staying in Ashford Court with friends of Hans. When can I see you?'

'It depends on when Mr Flateau takes me to London. Hoses Farm is quite a distance from you.'

'Hope to see you soon.' This re-union had to wait until I returned to London.

Hoses Farm

Hoses Farm became quite crowded at weekends when more

friends arrived, including John Strachey, who later became war minister, and Frank Owen, who was soon to become editor of the *Daily Mail*. More than a dozen congregated every weekend, all of whom were left-wing socialists. I found a serious discrepancy between their ideals and their style of living. Mrs Plummer paid the gardener £2 per week, the minimum Board of Trade wage. She gave him a cup of cocoa every morning – 'He doesn't have to pay for it,' she explained to us. Mr Plummer added: 'We also give him our old furniture. I saw him the other day in his cottage, sitting on our old settee as though he was somebody.'

Mr Plummer and his friends had been members of the Communist Party in the 1920s but had left to join the Labour Party. They were still very much influenced by the Party and what went on in the Soviet Union. Russia had signed a friendship pact with Germany and had declared the war to be 'imperialist'. The Communist Party of Britain campaigned for a 'People's Peace'. This caused tremendous discussion at Hoses Farm.

'Should we support the war, now that the workers' state has not joined in the fight?'

'But we wanted to fight fascism for years. How can we now ask for peace with the Nazis?'

'Surely, we can't ally ourselves with an ex-appeaser like Chamberlain.'

I wondered how anybody could want to make peace with Germany now. Only a couple of weeks ago they had all wanted to make war with Fascism. But I couldn't join in these conversations as my English wasn't good enough. In the end they all came to the obvious conclusion: it was a just war which all must support.

* * *

I was introduced to Jürgen Schulz, who told me: 'I'm recovering from a wound I received in the International Brigade in Spain.'

'Did you feel the odd man out as a German?' I asked.

'Oh no, there was a large German contingent. We sang songs from the concentration camps like *Die Moorsoldaten*.' He then broke into song.

'A large German contingent? How come?'

'You see, many anti-Nazi Germans who fled in 1933 volunteered.'

'I never knew that there were so many that they made up an entire contingent.'

'I want to introduce you to somebody else. Meet the last mayor of Madrid before its surrender to Franco.'

'Mr Plummer is a kind man,' this new acquaintance told me. 'He guaranteed for me to come to Britain.' The ex-mayor was short, with blond hair and an aquiline nose. In spite of his experiences the ex-mayor was happy and always joking.

* * *

During the week I often felt lonely, and used to go for long walks on my own in the countryside. My enforced idleness made me think of my mother and how I missed her, and I cried. But a 16 year-old boy mustn't cry so I was careful to wipe away my tears before I returned to the house. The almost daily letters had ceased; instead I received one Red Cross letter with 25 words every six months. I was not allowed to reply in my own handwriting. After the war my mother told me she thought I'd been injured in the bombing of London and lost my arms.

Leaving the Flateaus

Two weeks before Christmas 1939, Mr Flateau said: 'Would you like to spend a week with your family in London?'

'Yes please. I can meet my father.'

'Make a note of how much you spend during the week.' Upon my return to Hoses Farm I presented a bill of 18 shillings 3 ½ pence.

'Well done,' he said. 'From now on you can stay with your family permanently and we'll send you £1 per week.'

I didn't understand. 'Do you mean you want me to stay in London during the week and return at weekends?'

'No, I don't mean you to come back here at all. From now on you'll stay in London with your family permanently, and you can look for a job.'

Several minutes passed before I grasped the meaning of this. I went to my bedroom, sat on the bed and felt shattered. The Flateaus were my foster parents. I had lived with them for a whole year. I was used to their ways, and felt secure because I had a home. Now for the second time in 12 months I was homeless. My family couldn't help me – my father lived in a furnished room, like Onkel Jean and Tante Annie, while Hans and Gretel lived with their baby in very cramped conditions. They were paid for by Jewish charities.

Mr Flateau wrote to the Jewish Refugees Committee that due to the war he was unable to maintain his guarantee for me.

To me he said: 'We're sorry. Business is bad. We can't afford to keep you.'

It took me a very long time to get over the shock and disillusionment of the Flateaus' rejection. At that time I happened to read J.J. Rousseau's *Confessions*. The description of his feelings when he, alone, was abandoned by his 'maman' concurred with my own, and I devoured the book, comforted by the similarity of our emotions.

A week before Christmas I moved from Hoses Farm. The boys' hostel of the B'nai Brith, a Jewish Lodge, had a vacancy, and although I wasn't a member I was allowed to stay there temporarily. So I moved to Finchley Road but then I fell ill with tonsillitis. A doctor came and said that due to the danger of infection in a boys' hostel I'd have to go to the New End Hospital in Hampstead. As I was recovering I received a letter from the B'nai Brith saying that one of their members had claimed my bed for his son, so I could not return to the hostel. I was to be discharged the following day so I asked to see the hospital matron.

'I'm afraid I don't know where to go tomorrow. Please read this letter.'

'Alright, you may stay here until your father has found somewhere for you to live.'

I was thankful, as I was afraid I would end up in the street. At the hostel I only had a bed and a locker, so in hospital I was not worse off. Eventually the Refugee Children's Committee found me a place in one of their hostels in Primrose Hill, Chalk Farm.

Hostel Life

Churchill had become Prime Minister and this news electrified me. Since 1935 when he had warned the world about German re-armament, he had become Hitler's Public Enemy No.1. Hitler could not make a single speech without vilifying Churchill, and now he was Prime Minister. Throughout the war I felt elated whenever Churchill was mentioned. This was Britain's darkest hour, but to me Churchill made victory a certainty.

Mrs Dudley was the matron of the hostel in Primrose Hill. She was not an employee of the Jewish Refugees Committee but they paid her 17 shillings 6 pence per week for each boy. In order to make a profit, she had to save on food.

'Peter,' warned one of the boys, 'be careful with the jam this morning, it is running like mad.' Water had been added to the jam to make it last longer. At work jam sandwiches were difficult to eat because they kept on dripping all over the place.

On Saturdays and Sundays I went to weekend classes at the Sir John Cass Institute, Jewry Street. When the teacher saw me eating my sandwiches he said: 'Peter, take this sandwich. It's too much for me.' I always felt hungry. I often stopped in front of bakeries looking at the display of cakes, wondering if I would ever afford to buy one.

Mrs Dudley was a giant woman with a tremendous bosom. She used to shout at us because she thought it was the best way to make foreigners understand English. Her husband was a tiny man. He helped her and she treated him like a slave. At dinner time a girl was employed to serve the food. On one occasion she slipped and broke a plate.

'You damned fool!' Mrs Dudley screamed at her. 'Why can't you be more careful! You are useless!'

Her husband interjected: 'Please Lily, she didn't mean it. It was an accident.'

Mrs Dudley looked at him furiously. Her eyes were bulging. She approached him menacingly and he gazed at her anxiously. She raised her arm and walloped him on the cheek with such ferocity that it resounded throughout the dining room.

'That'll teach you!' she said.

When Mr Dudley had recovered, all he could say was: 'I told you before not to do such a thing in front of the boys.' Now we knew that such an event had occurred before. Her treatment of her husband was a source of tremendous amusement to us boys.

As enemy aliens were not allowed to operate the radio, only Mrs Dudley could turn it on. One day she saw us listening to a concert. 'I've told you before, you can't turn on the wireless on your own.'

'But it's only a symphony by Mozart.'

'I don't care what art it is.'

Her hostel also housed colonial students. I became friendly with Lahiri, an Indian law student.

'You love Britain, don't you?' he would mock me.

I resented this. 'After having lived in Germany you would appreciate Britain as well.'

'But you haven't lived in India. We're treated like Jews in our own country.'

'I don't think you know what a concentration camp is like.'

'I'll never be able to make you understand what British colonialism is like. It's just like the German rule over Europe.'

Prince Kessie of Ashanti, the nephew of the King of Ashanti, was another student caught up in England because of the war.

'Peter, I'm frightened.'

'Why, what's the matter?'

'They've caught up with me.'

'Who has?'

'The British secret service.'

'What do you mean?'

'Have a look at this letter.' It was addressed to His Royal Highness, Prince Kessie. The letter asked him to meet the writer for tea at a private address.

'Who is this man?'

'He's a brigadier. All colonials who hold prominent positions at home like myself are attached to an officer of the Colonial Office, ostensibly to help us but really to spy on us.'

'But you've nothing to hide.'

'The other day I gave a speech at the students union criticizing British colonialism and now they want to kill me.'

'I think you're exaggerating. Nobody wants to kill you.'

'In my last place I ran a bath and then I went back to my room to fetch some soap. When I returned to the bathroom a man left quickly and just said 'sorry'. The bath water had some black substance in it. He had tried to poison me.'

'Did you catch him?'

'No, I never saw him again. I left the place immediately and came here hoping nobody would find me because so many Jewish refugees live here. But they have found me.'

'I'm sure you're wrong. The British aren't like that.'

'I'm afraid you're mistaken. Lahiri is quite right.'

* * *

At home, as well as at work, I was a firewatcher. I had to stay up all night on a rota basis to report any fires during air raids. One evening during an air raid we were playing cards. Suddenly we heard the whistling of a falling bomb. Before we could duck under the table, the building shook, soot came through the fireplace and the lights went out. We rushed into the street and less than 100 yards away in Adelaide Road a direct hit had demolished a building. A woman was screaming: 'Someone is trapped!' Flames shot up from the house. I shattered the glass from a fire alarm and within seconds the fire brigade arrived.

On another occasion a shower of firebombs fell on Primrose Hill Road. An ARP warden was busy extinguishing them with a fire extinguisher. I started to kick the small incendiaries away from our house. 'Don't do that,' shouted the warden. Strangely, I didn't care that the bombs might explode.

* * *

We hated living in the hostel, but looking back on it, life there was at least not boring. As soon as I could afford it, I moved out and took a room with my father in Anson Road, Cricklewood, NW2. My father was now a nightwatchman. When he arrived home in the morning I had left for work. In the evening he was gone when I came home. If anything important happened we arranged to leave notes.

Mrs Landau

Mrs Landau lived in the house opposite ours. She was Austrian and kept a boarding house for boys from Germany, Austria, Czechoslovakia and Poland. She was a short, plump, motherly woman with a moustache. She spoke German with a heavy Viennese accent and could only converse in broken English. On Sundays Vati and I went to her place for lunch. She felt sorry for those of us who lived in bedsits. She welcomed any young people who dropped in, so whenever I felt at a loose end, in the evenings or at weekends, I ventured across the road. I entered a spacious but sparsely furnished home, and I felt warmth. The large kitchen, full of the familiar smell of continental cooking, was the main meeting place. As I entered I would be greeted and given a cup of real Viennese coffee. Other visitors and boarders would be seated around the table. The coffee pot stood in the middle and we helped ourselves. As we drank it Mrs Landau brewed a fresh pot. There were always heated discussions about the news:

'Have you heard the latest?'

'No, I missed the nine o'clock news.'

'The Russians have closed the loop at Stalingrad.'

'Thank God for that!'

Mrs Landau would introduce a newcomer: 'This is Alex. He's just arrived from Portugal.'

'How did you get here?'

'I was lucky. I've a cousin in Manchester. That's how I got a visa.'

'What's it like in Portugal?'

'Portugal is neutral, but the people are pro-Allies. All the taxi drivers wear Union Jacks in their lapels.'

A newcomer was always introduced by Mrs Landau mentioning his special interests: 'He's studying economics', 'he works for the BBC Overseas Service', 'you know, he fought in Spain'. Immediately we would take up the lead and discuss his experiences and make him feel at home.

As the Red Army advanced towards Germany, the Russians became very popular and Communism was respectable for a time.

'The Russians are the only ones who can fight.'

'Rubbish, once the second front is established we'll be just as good.'

'Why isn't there a second front?'

'Because we aren't ready.'

'Nonsense, we want the Russians to bleed to death, so that capitalism will triumph.'

'You're talking through your hat.'

And so it went on until late. I was lucky as I only had to cross the road to go to bed for I had to get up early. Mrs Landau would sit up and enjoy the conversation. She never took part, and I doubt whether she really followed our arguments, but she was pleased that her house was a place where we could relax and forget our anxieties for a time. She treated all of us as part of a large family. To allow the maximum number of boys to live in the house, she gave up her own bedroom and slept on a couch in the dining room. When several of 'her' family were interned she sent them food parcels. If anyone went to hospital she organized regular visits and always sent a present. She wasn't paid to do this – it was always her own money.

One evening I was sitting in her kitchen when Fred entered. He ran a clothing factory in Bond Street and I had been employed there for a time. He was a Czech refugee from Prague. I thought I'd amuse everybody when I related what went on in his factory. Surely he would see the joke, I thought.

'As soon as I came into Fred's factory,' I said, 'I rushed to the lavatory to read the morning paper. I stayed there for at least half an hour. Then I passed the paper to my mate who would spend the next half an hour there.' Everyone had a good laugh and Fred seemed to join in. The next day Mrs Landau said to me: 'You know, Fred was furious what you told about the goings on his factory. You humiliated him. Don't do anything like that again.'

* * *

By the end of the war most of us had joined the armed forces. One went back to Czechoslovakia with the Czech army – he escaped to England just in time after the Communist coup. Another joined Haganah and helped to establish the State of

Israel. Another was in hospital severely wounded and permanently disabled. I visited him until he died. Some had emigrated to the United States. Others, like myself, studied in order to enter the professions.

Those of us who stayed in this country applied for British citizenship. Mrs Landau didn't, and one day a policeman arrived and the following conversation took place.

'Why don't you apply to become British?'

'I'm happy as I am.'

'But when you're British you won't have to register with the police and you won't need a special licence to run a boarding house.'

'You know me very well. I'm not bothering you in any way. I'm an old woman and can hardly speak English. I don't want to become English. Please leave me alone.'

The police left her alone.

* * *

Eight years after the war, while studying for my degree at Hull, I decided to visit Mrs Landau in order to introduce my fiancée, Sylvia. A stranger opened the door and informed me that she had died. The place was now a boarding house for the elderly and none of the boarders could remember her.

'Mrs Landau wasn't ill,' I was told. 'She went to bed as usual and in the morning she was found dead.' The new matron told me this while I was sitting in the kitchen at the same table where we had had those wonderful conversations over cups of Viennese coffee.

I said goodbye to the new matron, sad that I would never again visit the house in Anson Road.

14 *Friendly Enemy Aliens*

It is June 1940 and the BBC announces: 'The government has decided to intern all German nationals, this includes those who came to this country as refugees.'

When war broke out we had to appear before a tribunal. We were officially declared to be 'Friendly Enemy Aliens' and were not to be interned. However when France fell the government panicked. Most refugees felt very bitter about the government's U-turn but I didn't. My job as a tailor's apprentice was so boring that I believed an internment would be a welcome break. My packed suitcase was standing ready for the policeman's call.

It came on 26 June 1940, my seventeenth birthday. A jovial-looking policeman arrived at 7.30 a.m.

'Is Peter Prager here?' he asked.

'Yes,' I replied, my face gleaming.

'I'm afraid you have to come with me to Albany Street Barracks in order to proceed to an internment camp. You have one hour to pack your things.'

'Can I take my tennis racket along?' I asked.

'Of course,' the policeman replied. 'You will be able to go in for all sorts of sports. After all, you'll have nothing to do there.' Later I found out that this was sheer invention.

* * *

I had been in England for 18 months and I spoke fluent English. However I had not yet learnt the intricacies of English conventions. There is no German equivalent for addressing somebody as 'sir'. This omission in my English education was to provide me soon with new headaches.

In the huge courtyard of Albany Street Barracks, where I was taken by police car, were dozens of tables and a queue of people to be interviewed. A sergeant stood behind each officer at the table.

When my turn came the officer said: 'Put all your valuables on the table.'

I didn't have much, just a watch and a few shillings.

'Is this all?' the officer asked.

'Yes,' I replied.

The officer gave me a stern look. 'Have you not forgotten something?'

I emptied my pockets, looked around me but did not see anything I might have forgotten. 'No,' I replied.

The sergeant whispered in my ear: 'You must always say yes sir or no sir.'

'Yes sir.'

The officer looked at my papers. 'Have you got a passport?' he asked.

I was so tense that I forgot the sergeant's advice. 'No.'

The officer gave me a furious look. 'What did you say?' he asked.

The sergeant in a louder whisper said: 'Please say, no sir.'

I replied immediately: 'No, sir.'

'That's better,' the officer said. Now the officer asked me for my next-of-kin. I told him my brother's and father's address.

'Any other relations?'

'No,' I replied again, forgetting the important 'sir'. The officer stared at me for a few seconds. No doubt he was thinking: 'here is one of those cunning Germans who is trying to outwit me by being deliberately obstructive.' The officer was turning red and his eyes began to bulge. Any minute there was going to be an explosion.

The sergeant, who was well meaning, became quite desperate. 'Please, do say sir,' he pleaded with me.

'Oh, I am sorry, I mean no sir.'

It was too late. The officer had lost his temper. He was screaming at me: 'Don't worry, my lad, when you come out of here you'll know how to behave. We'll teach you manners yet!'

I was beginning to get worried, perhaps internment was not a kind of holiday camp.

After the interrogation we were taken by coach to Lingfield racecourse which had been turned into an internment camp.

A sergeant received us: 'Here's a mattress cover and there's straw. Take as much straw as you like to make yourselves comfortable. Over there, do you see the stables? That's where you'll sleep.'

As we walked towards the stables we were overtaken by ambulances. 'Anyone fallen ill?' I asked a guard. He replied: 'They are our internees brought in from local hospitals. They're taken straight to our first aid post.' It seemed these stretcher cases also presented a danger to the realm.

Of course all of us spoke German, but to my amazement I noticed a small group standing in a circle and speaking English with a cockney accent, seemingly more dismal and bewildered than the rest of us.

I approached one of them and said: 'I can see you are not German. What on earth are you doing here?'

'Well, you see,' he replied, 'fifty years ago England was short of clerks. So they got hold of Germans to work for them.' Pointing to his mates, he continued: 'Our parents came from all over Germany. I can't remember anything about Germany because I was three when I arrived. My father was interned during the last war. We never bothered to get naturalized. And here we are now.'

The camp commander called a meeting for all inmates. 'I have asked you to come here so that you can organize yourselves and establish some sort of entertainment programme. You don't want to die of boredom do you?' This was meant to be funny, but none of us laughed.

At the end of the meeting, the camp doctor, a fellow internee, suggested: 'To finish, let us sing, *Roll out the Barrel*.' It was a goodwill gesture towards the commander who was sitting amongst us, but we unanimously decided that we didn't feel like it.

The camp had been used by POWs before we came. They had been transferred to another camp except for two sailors. One of them was Vogel, the other was called Horst.

'You see,' explained Vogel to me, 'I come from Bremen and we like the English. We hated the Nazis. When I told my fellow prisoners I thought England would win the war and then we could get rid of Hitler, they set on me and Horst and beat us up.' He showed me his face which had a big scar.

'That's the result of the beating. Horst and I had to be protected. So when they moved the POWs to another camp to prepare this one for the Jews, they thought we would be happier with you. And so we are.'

Vogel was in charge of the kitchen chores and he asked if I would like to help in the kitchen. I immediately agreed as I did not want to remain idle all day long. Our food was monotonous but adequate. In the kitchen there was a special section for the guards. It was fenced off but we could see all the goodies which we did not have: ham, bacon and eggs, sausages, jam, butter and buns. When we had finished washing up in the evenings, Vogel would climb over the fence and fetch food for a late-night snack. Eventually the mess sergeant became suspicious and said the matter of missing food must be investigated. It looked as though we would be found out. To avert this, Vogel said to the mess sergeant: 'I've got an idea which will stop the thief.'

'Well, what is it?' asked the mess sergeant.

'The fence is not high enough. Put some barbed wire along the top. That'll stop them.'

'Splendid idea.' he said. 'You'd better get on with it straight away.'

The task was finished faultlessly. The C.O. inspected the job: 'Vogel,' he said, 'I must congratulate you. The kitchen really is more secure now. I don't know what we would do without you.'

Vogel had succeeded in diverting suspicion away from him, but I was sorry that this stopped our late-night snacks.

We ate in two dining halls. The smaller one was used for Orthodox Jews who ate kosher meals. The majority used the larger one and we could not make the authorities understand that we were also Jews.

One of our fellow internees was the pianist Franz Osborn, at the time one of the best pianists living in England. Because he had connections with Members of Parliament he was released after only two weeks. A week later he visited us again, a free man, to give us a special recital of Beethoven's *Apassionata*.

The weather was hot and when we were not working we were lounging on the racecourse sleeping. We all felt very languid. Rumour had it that bromide was put into our food to reduce sexual desires though this was against the Geneva Convention.

After a month I was transferred to Huyton, Liverpool, where I met my brother. Food tasted infinitely better in this camp, but during the second night of my stay almost all inmates suffered a severe attack of diarrhoea. An investigation showed that we had been supplied with meat which had been condemned by the Liverpool health authorities as unfit for human consumption.

The next day the following announcement was pinned on the notice board: 'Tomorrow afternoon representatives from the International Red Cross will visit the camp to hear any complaints which any inmates wish to make.' It was explained to us that they were the representatives of the German government. The Red Cross arrived but none of us came forward with a complaint. We would not have the German government represent us for anything.

A further announcement appeared: 'It is proposed to set up a camp university. Will any teachers, university lecturers, artists or anybody else who can contribute to such a project please report to Hut no.4.'

Meanwhile the government was severely criticized for its internment policy in Parliament. As a result those under 18 were released immediately. Thus, I arrived back in London just in time for the London Blitz. I was back in my boring job, none the worse for my experience.

My brother, together with thousands of other internees, joined the British army straight from the internment camp. Soon he was accepted for OCTU and was subsequently commissioned. I have never been able to understand the thinking behind interning someone because he cannot be trusted and then within a short space of time giving him a commission which is a position of trust.

15   Starting Work

December 1939, Cricklewood Industrial Estate, 7.30 a.m. I stand in a big square shivering in the cold drizzle. I am wearing only a thin raincoat given free by Marks & Spencer to all refugee children. People are streaming towards the factories. I see someone who looks like a manager.

'I'm a refugee. Have you got a job?' I had been doing this for three days.

The man looks at me sympathetically: 'Follow me.' In his office he says: 'I'm also a refugee.'

'Ah, good.'

'You know you said the wrong thing.'

'Why?'

'Never say you're a refugee. People don't like it.'

'What should I say?'

'Never mind that now. I'll help you.'

'That's marvellous.'

'We manufacture light bulbs. Would you be willing to sit in front of a machine all day manipulating bulbs?'

'Of course I would. I'll do anything. I need a job.'

'All right. I'll give you a letter for the labour exchange asking for a work permit. You can start tomorrow.'

I was happy. The next day I went to the juvenile employment bureau. There were five boys and three girls waiting to see the employment officer. I entered the office. The man who interviewed me was middle aged and pleasant enough. As he read my future employer's letter he shook his head.

'So you want to work as an engineering apprentice?'

'Yes, the firm wants me to start immediately.'

'Are you aware that we have 300 British juveniles on our books?'

'No, I didn't know.'

'Well we have.'

'I see. What does this mean?' I became anxious.

'We'll have to place our British boys first. Then we can see to you.'

'When will that be?'

'In about a year.'

My face dropped. 'But I need a job now.'

'Are you willing to take any job?'

'Yes of course.'

'We can send you to the West End. Do you mind the tailoring trade?'

'Any job will do.'

'Alright, we can fix you up then.'

This was the start of my tailoring career. I thought my mother would approve. German Jews had been doctors, lawyers, academics and businessmen, but the world didn't want intellectuals. They needed engineers, agricultural workers – people who worked with their hands. Mutti wanted me 'to do something practical, something with your hands'. She was so traumatized by the persecution of Jews that she thought it would continue for ever. Tailoring was something 'to do with your hands'.

Tailoring

L. Bloom, Tottenham Mews, W1, £1 per week. It was a tailoring workshop with 20 employees. For the first time I came into contact with Jews of East European origin. Many of them used Yiddish expressions, and Yiddish was unknown to me. Mr Field, the manager, was a young fellow with jovial manners. He introduced me to the workers:

'This is Peter. We had to take him because he was the only one the labour exchange sent. It's on account of the war.' I didn't think this was much of an introduction.

Then he explained: 'The first thing you do in the morning is to sweep the floor. Pick up any pins in the process – we don't waste anything. Then make tea. Ask each worker what they want for lunch and go out and get it. After lunch you take the finished coats to our wholesaler and bring back the cloth. If you have more than 20 garments you can take a taxi.'

'I thought I was going to learn the trade.'

'Oh yes, you will. During the slack period. At the moment we're rather busy and the workers have no time to teach you. They're all on piece work.'

The workers recounted to me what the conditions were like in the old days. 'Before the last war,' an elderly worker told me, 'the boss made us work as long as the gaslight was burning. "It's the law," he said. We believed him because rules like this did exist in Russia. Then he would disappear and put another shilling in the meter.'

After 12 months I received a rise of 2 shillings and 3 pence. I had learned nothing and decided to leave. I worked in many small tailoring workshops after that and loathed every minute.

L. Harris

I was given a chance to learn something at a large factory, L. Harris, makers of Harella coats. I was trained to be a cutter. I started cutting linings and then advanced to cloth.

One day I was given the job of cutting 26 layers of cloth for 26 coats. By mistake I cut the sleeves too short. I didn't know what to do. If the manager found out I knew I'd get the sack. I looked around to see whether anybody could see me. I took a bale of cloth and decided to cut 26 new sleeves. Still nobody took any notice of me. I cut up the short sleeves and put them into the sack for waste cloth. When the roll of cloth was finished they'd be ten yards short. But this wouldn't be for several days and by then it would be impossible to find out who had used too much cloth.

Three days later a cutter said to the foreman: 'I'm ten yards short.' The foreman told the manager, the manager told the boss, and the boss phoned the manufacturer. The manufacturer's representative arrived and he started unrolling and measuring every bale supplied by him. That morning chaos reigned in the cutting room. I carried on as though nothing untoward had happened. All the cloth measured was correct. The mystery remained unsolved.

* * *

The management of L. Harris didn't believe in trade unions. Any worker suspected of recruiting for the National Union of Tailors and Garment Workers was immediately dismissed. As we left the factory our bags were searched for subversive leaflets. A leaflet was found on me and I was called to the manager's office.

'Are you recruiting for the union?'

'Yes, I am.'

'I ought to dismiss you. I'm surprised that you as a foreigner engage in politics.' The manager himself was a refugee.

'I didn't know that union membership has anything to do with politics.'

'Yes it has. I've noticed you read books during break. You're an intelligent boy. As a Jew you should occupy yourself with Jewish affairs, not English politics. If you persist in union activities, your chance of learning the trade is nil. Here's something for you to read.' He passed me a copy of the *Zionist Review*. 'It's better than your union trash.'

I went back to the cutting room. I read the paper with interest and showed a poignant article to Sid the foreman.

The next day I was called again to the manager. 'You haven't heeded my advice.'

'Yes, I have.'

'But only yesterday you showed Sid some communist propaganda.'

'No I haven't. I showed him an article from the *Zionist Review* which you gave me. I've still got it upstairs.'

The manager became confused. Sid, like many other Jews who came to this country from Russia before the First World War, was illiterate. I did not know this. 'All right you can go back to your work bench.'

I was furious. I rushed back, confronted Sid and shouted at the top of my voice. 'You stool pigeon, you lout, you illiterate idiot, you don't know the difference between this paper (I held the *Zionist Review* under his nose) and a communist paper. Why don't you go back to school and learn to read?' I made so much noise that the other workers switched off their machines to listen to what was going on. I knew I was in the right and could not be sacked for this. Sid said nothing, and the next day he was absent.

The following day there was an announcement over the factory radio: 'We regret to announce that Sid the cutting room foreman has died of a heart attack. He had had a heart condition for some time.'

As is the Jewish custom, prayers were said for Sid for the entire week. A minimum of ten Jewish men are required for this and they were short of a tenth man. I was asked to join.

The firm stopped training me, and a few weeks later I left.

The Bike

I was cycling to work along Albany Street towards the Euston Road behind an army lorry when suddenly the lorry stopped. It tried to back into a sidestreet. The driver hadn't seen me and it looked as though he was going to crash into me. I was just able to get off my bike when the back of the lorry went over it. The big wheels of the lorry completely squashed my bike which now looked like a flattened Mickey Mouse in a Walt Disney film. The accident took place outside a police station. I leant the bike against the railings of the station and went to work.

On my way back I intended to pick up the bike. A policeman called: 'Will you come in please?' I entered the police station.

'Is this your bicycle?'

'Yes, it is.'

'Why did you leave it outside the police station?'

'The accident happened right here.'

'Yes, but why did you leave it here?'

'I couldn't carry it and as I had to go to work I had to leave it here.'

'You didn't secure it. There is a chain and a lock but you didn't lock it.'

I thought the policeman was joking. 'I didn't think anybody would steal this bike,' I said laughingly, pointing to its squashed wheels.

'Did you know we had to employ an officer all day to watch over your property?' He was dead serious.

I became worried and changed my manner. 'I am so sorry, sir, I know I was rather careless.'

'So you were. We don't want to employ officers for this sort of unnecessary work.'

'No, of course you don't.'

'Don't do anything like this again.'

'No sir, I won't. I promise.'

'Alright. You can go.'

I carried the bike home.

16   The Free German Youth

I am sitting in a Bakerloo Line train going home from the City to Willesden Green. Opposite me sits a girl and I wonder if I know her. The girl stares at me intently as if she knows me.

Suddenly she gets up: 'Are you Peter?'

'You are Bobby!' We shake hands.

'It's more than ten years since we saw each other in Berlin.'

'I think it is.'

'Where are you going?'

'Home. And you?'

'I'm on my way to the Free German Youth. Have you heard of us?'

'Only a little.'

'It's an organization of German refugees fighting fascism. We meet to discuss current affairs. You must come. I know you'll like it. What are you doing tonight?'

'Nothing in particular.'

'Come along. We have our group evening tonight. We meet at 8 o'clock.'

'O.K. I'll be there.'

So I went to the meeting and was immediately greeted: 'Hello Peter, welcome. Bobby told us you were coming.'

Bobby introduced me. 'This is Horst Brasch. He's the chairman.'

The Free German Youth was a communist front organization recruiting young German Jewish refugees. They intended to indoctrinate us and send us to a communist Germany after the war. Horst Brasch was a non-Aryan Catholic whose Jewish parents had had him baptized. He came to England in a kindertransport as a 16 year-old. He was of medium build with a pleasant looking face and a perpetual smile. I wondered how such an affable boy could be a hardheaded communist. (After the war he became Minister of Culture in the DDR.)

'Welcome Peter, I'm pleased you've come. We need new members.'

'This is Marianne. She lives here.'

'Hello, I'll get you a coffee.'

'Thanks.'

'Where do you live?'

'Anson Road.'

'That's good. It's just round the corner.'

I felt something that I had not felt since I left my parent's home – that I belonged. We were about 20 teenagers and we all sat in a circle. The group leader welcomed me and hoped I would join the group permanently. Then the German communist workers' song, *Volk ans Gewehr* was sung. I would have preferred an English song. The evening started in earnest. The subject was Brecht. Who is he? I had never heard of him. A piece of his was read out called 'Longheads and Roundheads.' It ridiculed Nazi racial theory and struck a chord. I recalled the time my teacher had measured my head at the Grunewald Gymnasium. This dramatic piece was read out in parts by several members and it was enthralling. The meeting was closed after an hour with the singing of the Soviet Fatherland song, which has the refrain: 'There is no country in the entire world where the heart beats so free.' Singing in the group was important. It bound us together and the text helped to cement our beliefs. After some more chatting we hurried home because as enemy aliens we were all subjected to permanent curfew. I became a member.

After the meeting Bobby said: 'You must visit me. Can you come tomorrow?'

'Alright, I'll come.'

I felt lonely and was glad of the invitation. This was my first visit to a girl's room. It was known that the Free German Youth believed in free love, a practice very much frowned upon by the outside world. I thought this meant girls went to bed with anyone. How was I to behave when I visited her? I went to her room with some trepidation. I knew she lived with her boy friend. Where was he?

'Jochen is out,' she explained.

This put me in a quandary. Was it an invitation for sex? It must be. I'd never had sex before – an opportunity not to be missed. I was nervous and excited. Does she really want me to seduce her? I was dithering.

'Here's a cup of coffee, Peter.' She gave it to me and sat in the middle of her bed – the only piece of furniture in the room.

I sat on the edge of the bed. 'You know, Marxism is discredited,' I said.

'Nonsense,' she replied.

'Remember the Berlin transport workers' strike in 1932?'

'What of it?' she asked.

I moved a bit nearer. 'If the communists had not joined up with the Nazis, the government would not have fallen.' Triumphantly I moved another inch towards the middle.

Bobby noticed my movement and moved an inch away from me. 'You are misinformed,' she assured me. 'The transport workers were solidly behind the Party. The Nazis had no influence whatever.' She watched to see if I moved any closer.

I thought she was being coy.

'The Party called the Social Democrats social fascists. This split the workers' movement.' I had scored again and moved another couple of inches.

'Von Papen was the real culprit,' Bobby said angrily and moved further away. By now she had reached the edge of the bed – another inch and she would fall off.

'If the Party had looked to Germany instead of Moscow there would never have been a Nazi government,' I said. I didn't know what to do next. Confused thoughts flashed through my mind.

'You're just repeating bourgeois propaganda,' she replied. Her entire body was perched on the edge, and she held herself up with one arm which touched the floor while I had shifted to the middle. A crisis point had been reached.

I knew I had to do something, even if it ended with my humiliation. Suddenly there was a noise outside, then the front door opened.

'Hello Jochen!' Bobby exclaimed.

He entered the room and she gave him a quick kiss.

'Well, did you convert Peter?'

'Not quite,' I answered. I thanked Bobby for the coffee and left.

* * *

In May 1941 we were to meet an English youth club. Hans, our group leader, gave us instructions: 'We must show solidarity and speak with one voice. We must tell them that the German people are seething with revolt against fascism. The German army is the German people. They will start the revolt. Britain must give a lead. We are supposed to be at war with Germany but the government really sympathizes with fascism and is not fighting the war properly.'

'What rubbish!' I thought.

The English youth club was situated in Willesden in a church in mock-Tudor style. We were sitting in a room with windows which looked sixteenth century. John, their leader, was a fair young man in his twenties. He spoke with an educated English accent which contrasted sharply with our German accent. The members were in their late teens like us.

John welcomed us. 'We want to have closer contact with the refugee community. That's why we have invited you.'

Hans replied: 'We want to give you our views on the present political situation.' But the club members preferred cuddling to politics. The club was the only opportunity for them to be away from their parents. Hans continued: 'The German workers are waiting to revolt against the war.'

He waited for comments from the English members. Instead I got up. 'Nonsense, we just saw the repatriation of wounded German POWs on the newsreel. As they boarded the ship they greeted the camera with the Nazi salute. Even those carried on a stretcher raised their right arm. The shock of their injuries hasn't brought them to their senses. They will never rise against their government.'

Our members were shocked by my outburst. How dare I oppose the Party line? However, it didn't matter what we said, as our hosts were too busy kissing and cuddling. Their embarrassed leader replied: 'We see your point.'

After the meeting Hans turned on me: 'Peter, you are a political ignoramus. You've spoilt the evening.'

* * *

At one of our group evenings I gave a talk on George Bernard Shaw. I concluded: 'Thanks to Shaw and his friends in the Fabian Society the Labour Party became reformist. They were totally against revolution.'

Hans smiled condescendingly: 'You forgot to mention that Shaw was really a Marxist. He had a picture of Karl Marx hanging in his study. You didn't refer to his friendly visits to the Soviet Union either.'

* * *

In 1943, 90,000 Germans were taken prisoner in Stalingrad. The BBC radio announced: 'Fieldmarshal von Paulus, General von Seydlitz and other German officers together with communist exiles have formed a Free German Committee in Moscow. This Committee has asked the German people to rise against their government.'

At our next group evening Hans said: 'We have just sent off a telegram affiliating to the Moscow Committee.'

'How can you do this without consulting us first?' I asked.

'All of us want the German people to revolt.'

'But we're Jews. Can you imagine the Germans taking the slightest notice of us?'

'We are anti-fascists first.'

'As a Jew I want nothing to do with German organizations. Even if they want to rise against the Nazis, to me they are Germans and I don't want to join them.'

With such views, how could I remain a member of the Free German Youth? About a dozen of us felt the same and we left.

I received a letter from Horst Brasch, the Chairman. 'We are sorry to note that you have abandoned the fight against fascism.'

Years later I met a defected leading member. He told me: 'We had many discussions about you. We considered expulsion but decided against it because you represented an important bourgeois element and your presence would attract others. When you left of your own accord, we felt we had failed.'

17   The Jewish Youth Group

The following day several of us saw Dr Werner Rosenstock, General Secretary of the Association of Jewish Refugees. We told him that we wanted to start our own Jewish group, and wished to meet socially to discuss things. We asked him if he could help. Our idea was to integrate into British society instead of preparing to return to Germany.

'We're pleased you left the Free German Youth. We don't like our youth becoming involved in communism. We'll help you form your own group. Come back next week and I'll see what we can do for you.'

A few days later we were told: 'We've booked a room at 1 Broadhurst Gardens. We've paid a month's rent for one evening per week. After that you'll have to finance it yourselves.'

This was the start of the Jewish Youth Group. 'I think you need to boost your membership,' Dr Rosenstock said to me some time later. 'The publisher Victor Gollancz is interested in young people. He's agreed to speak at a public meeting to recruit members for non-communist youth clubs. He feels strongly about the 10,000 children who came here without their parents and who must feel very lonely.'

The meeting was held on a Sunday at Conway Hall. Victor Gollancz spoke first: 'I say to the British government, open the doors of Palestine! Let my people go! Give them a chance to escape from the hell of Europe! Meanwhile those of you who are in this country will, I hope, join the various youth clubs assembled in this hall.' Apart form us, there were speakers from Hashomer Hatzair, Habonim and Mizrachi.

I spoke first: 'Many of you do not feel Zionist but would nevertheless like to belong to a Jewish youth organization. If you feel like this, join us. We meet every Monday night at eight o'clock and hope to provide an interesting programme, and we have lots of discussions on almost every subject.'

Our meetings were held in a large room with about 30 chairs and one big table. There was no other furniture. I was elected chairman and introduced the speakers. We spoke English, while at the Free German Youth all business was conducted in German.

Our guest speakers included Captain Fisher of the US Army, talking about the American Constitution, and Rabbi Van Der Zyl speaking about Jewish festivals. This talk was followed by a member of the Russia Today Society on Russia. The most interesting talk was given by a member of Hashomer Hatzair: 'We are Marxist and want to build a socialist Palestine in which Arabs and Jews can live together in complete equality. We believe in a bi-national state.'

'How can you be Marxist if you are Jewish? The two don't go together.'

'We reject religion. We are secular Jews.' This was a concept new to me.

'If you want to see how we live you can spend your week's annual holiday with us. We work on a farm in the Malvern Hills and live in a kibbutz the same way we'll live in Eretz Israel.' I took up the offer. 'All the wages we earn we pool and everybody gets exactly the same.'

'This is communism in practice,' I said.

'Yes, it is. And this is the society we intend to build in Palestine.'

A few months later the kibbutz decided to move to London. They took jobs and created an urban egalitarian society. One night in an air raid their house received a direct hit and most of them were killed.

The meetings of the Jewish Youth Group finished at 9.30 when I announced: 'We've got to finish. Let's transfer to the Cosmo Café.' The café was situated in Finchley Road where excellent continental coffee was served, rare in those days. Now there was more light-hearted talk.

Freddy Loewe was one of our members. He had a nervous twitch which at times disconcerted us. 'You're lucky, you managed to come here with your sister and your parents.'

'I don't think so.'

'Why?'

'I'll tell you. We left Germany in 1939 in the *St Louis*, bound for the United States. The boat carried only Jewish refugees many of whom, including my father, had been in concentration camps. As we approached the US coast there was an announcement from the ship's loudspeaker: "Unfortunately the US authorities will not allow you to land because, they say, your papers are not in order. Don't worry, we'll take you to Cuba where the government will be more accommodating." We became rather apprehensive. We wanted to go to the US, but anything was better than Germany. However, Cuba also refused. No country was willing to accept us so the captain was forced to sail back to Germany. The ship turned and we sailed across the Atlantic eastward. When this happened my mother and sister started to cry and my father turned white. Then I heard people shouting and screaming and hadn't noticed that my father had disappeared. Suddenly a friend came rushing towards us: "Your father has jumped into the ocean." At the same time a voice over the loudspeaker shouted: "Man overboard!" The ship's engines screeched to a halt. I ran to the railings. A lifeboat was lowered and I saw my father being hauled into the boat. He was semi-conscious and recovered slowly. Finally we were given permission to land in England and went to Cambridge where we had friends. My father never recovered completely and died a few months later.'

After this tale it took some time until we could resume our conversation. But we were teenagers and soon we were able to laugh again. Freddy laughed loudest, then he started to scream. At first we took it for laughter but then we realized it was a nervous attack and we stopped laughing. We tried to soothe him by patting his back. When this didn't help we left the café with him so that he could breathe the calming fresh air.

* * *

When the war ended most of us, including Freddy, joined the US Army Intelligence Corps and went to Germany as postal censors and interpreters. Freddy and I were stationed in Offenbach. At weekends we hitchhiked to Heidelberg from where we could phone England. Freddy always phoned Evelyn, his girlfriend.

One day he said to me: 'Peter, I'm going home. I can't be without Evelyn. I want to marry her.'

'Can't you wait till your contract expires?'

'No, I can't. I can't live without her.'

'But the Americans won't let you go home.'

'I'll just tell them I can't read the letters. As I wear strong glasses they will have to believe me.'

They did and he returned to London. He married Evelyn and emigrated to America. He started a business and lived happily with Evelyn until he died a few years ago of a heart attack.

* * *

By November 1945, while I was working in Germany, membership of the Jewish Youth Group had diminished to such an extent that the Annual General Meeting could not attract a quorum. The few remaining members decided to disband.

18   Return to Germany

Coming Home
Muss man sich mit Wasser quälen,
Das kommt nur vom Hitler wählen,

Wir waren überall dabei
Wir drängten uns in die Partei.

Wir waren geringe Profitler,
Wir schrieen laut und oft 'Heil Hitler!'

Wir nannten 'Ihn' ein Höheres Wesen,
Doch 'Nazi' sind wir nie gewesen.

Because we always voted for Hitler
We now find that even water is rationed.

We wanted to participate in everything,
We clamoured to join the Nazi Party.

We profited by the regime,
We cried loud and often 'Heil Hitler!'

We thought 'Him' a divine person.
But Nazi, we have never been.

This poem was sent through the post and intercepted by me as
a postal censor in the US Civil Censorship Division, Frankfurt.

End of War

It is winter 1944 and I am glued to the radio. I listen to every
bulletin and I am so excited I can hardly sleep. Russian troops

enter Germany from the east. The Western Allies conquer Aachen in the west. The war cannot last long now.

On 20 April, Hitler's birthday, Soviet troops reach Berlin. The Russians have to fight for every street. Finally, the Red Flag is hoisted on the Reichstag.

A few months before the battle of Berlin, a Red Cross letter from Mutti arrives: 'Onkel Franz is in a military hospital.' How could that be? Surely they have not conscripted him into the army? Is he still alive?

On 4 July British and American troops entered Berlin. My brother Hans was among them. He wrote: 'Mutti and Onkel Franz are both alive and still live in their old flat. Onkel Franz was in a forced labour camp where he was beaten up. Both are in terrible shape. There is no food.'

I knew I just had to go to Berlin. The British were short of German-speaking personnel, so I applied to join the Intelligence Corps to be told that only British citizens were accepted. As the British didn't naturalize anybody during the war this was a classic Catch 22 situation.

Then a friend informed me that the Americans had opened a recruiting office at the top of the Marks & Spencer building in Oxford Street, and didn't care about your nationality. I went there and was given a reading test in German. I hadn't seen German for five years, and I failed. I was told to practise at home and come back the next week. This time I passed and was posted to Offenbach, near Frankfurt.

My first destination was Paris for an induction course. A sergeant instructed us on bed-making, telling us that it was very important that we make beds in US Army fashion. 'Can you see how we fold our blankets? Not at all like the British.' As I didn't know how to fold blankets the British way this didn't mean much to me. We were also taught that it was important to address officers correctly. As civilians in uniform we were to say: 'Yes, Captain' and 'No, Colonel'. The training lasted one week.

A Survivor's Story

In Paris I visited a Jewish family who survived the war living underground. They took me to their aunt who lived in the outskirts of the city. This is her story.

'We went underground during the occupation, my husband and my three girls. One day my husband was approached by a stranger. He promised to take the girls to North Africa, but it would cost a lot of money. We scraped the money together. My husband took our girls to the pre-arranged assembly point. The stranger waited with the Gestapo. I've never seen the four of them again.'

The woman showed me the girls' bedroom which she had left with the curtains drawn, beds unmade, in the same state as it was when they left two years ago. Then she took me to the town square. There on the war memorial were engraved the names of the husband and three children. She pointed to the names and said: 'That's all I have left.' She behaved like someone who was still in a dream. Then, as a memento, she gave me the yellow star she had been forced to wear.

Reaching Germany

On 4 September we crossed into Germany. In the middle of the night the train stopped for shunting. I heard voices: *Weiter rechts – ja so*. The speakers had a Frankfurt dialect. These first German sounds recalled the train journey from Berlin to Hamburg in December 1938, the Gestapo standing outside our carriage and the paralysing fear that gripped us children. I remember my promise that one day I would come back to Germany but in the uniform of an occupying army. A promise come fulfilled. We crossed the Rhine on a pontoon bridge because the retreating Germans had destroyed all bridges. Frankfurt was almost completely in ruins.

On my first free evening I walked through Offenbach to look at the town. Only a few buildings had been destroyed. I saw a pretty girl walking along. I offered her a cigarette and started a conversation.

'How have you fared under the occupation?'
'You are treating us abominably.'
'How come?'
'We haven't got enough to eat. And the bureaucracy!'
'What bureaucracy?'
'If we leave town we need a permit. A ration card from the next village is not valid here. If you've been a Party member

you're fired. My favourite teacher has lost his job because he's been in the Party.'

'What about the Jews? Have you ever thought how they've been treated?'

'That's different. During a war you intern your enemies. You did the same.'

'And Auschwitz?'

'That's Russian propaganda. They're trying to hide their own crimes. How is it you speak such good German?'

'I'm a German Jew.'

There was a long pause. She gave me a furious look and walked away. Most Germans assured me they had never been Nazis. 'We've always hated Hitler,' was their stock reply. I understood the bitter feelings of the writer of the poem at the beginning of the chapter. It had been sent from Berlin where public utility services had broken down. Even the water supply had ceased to function. A few days before his suicide, Hitler had given orders to flood the Berlin underground system drowning thousands of civilians who had taken refuge there. The polluted water mingled with the drinking water supply. Cholera broke out and the Germans had to queue for hours for pure drinking water – in summer, during a heat wave.

The reasoning for Hitler's orders were expressed by him during one of his table talks. 'I have always believed in the principle of the survival of the fittest. I thought the Germans were the fittest, destined to rule the world. Events have proved otherwise. The future belongs to the Russians. We Germans have no right to exist.'

While I was working at the main Frankfurt post office I was in charge of a section dealing with parcel censorship. Many parcels were sent by farmers destined for an internment camp for high-ranking Nazis. The parcels contained food and these Nazis seemed to be rather lucky to have such good friends. The German police regularly searched our workers in case of postal theft. One day the police reported to me that they had arrested one of my men for stealing a sausage. The man was in his fifties and a Sunday school teacher. He asked to go to the toilet before being taken to the police station. He climbed through the toilet window and threw himself into the courtyard and was killed. His widow told me that he had never before committed an offence and she knew that such humiliation would have been more than he could bear. I felt that if I had supervised the men more carefully this tragedy would not have happened. I found it impossible to wipe this man's death from my conscience.

On Friday nights I visited Rabbi Neuhaus. He had returned from Theresienstadt concentration camp and was officiating again in Frankfurt. Rabbi Neuhaus was in his early sixties. He was of medium height and fairly slim. He came from the German tradition of Liberal Judaism. Almost none of his former congregation had survived. His work consisted of serving the small community of displaced persons who originated from Eastern Europe. His wife was a well-rounded, lively 50-year-old. They both talked incessantly, which helped those of us who were too shy to say much. On Fridays he kept open house for visiting soldiers.

The Rabbi was preparing for emigration to California where his son lived. As a German citizen his luggage was limited and parcel services had not yet been established.

I said to Mrs Neuhaus: 'I'm quite willing to send your clothing through the army post.' This way I sent several parcels to her son. One day she gave me a heavy parcel.

'This is heavy.' I was concerned lest she gave me forbidden goods.

'I know,' she said. Her eyes showed that the parcel did contain something prohibited.

'It can't be clothes.'

'No, it isn't. It's prunes.'

'Prunes?' I thought she was joking, trying to cover up something else.

'Yes, prunes.'

'You mean you're sending prunes to California?' I couldn't believe it.

'You see, when we arrive in the States we'll be poor. We won't be able to buy anything. We don't want to be a burden on our son.'

'Yes, but prunes are so cheap in America.'

'The trouble is I can't live without prunes. I must eat them every day. And in America we'll be paupers.'

I didn't know whether to laugh or cry. 'I can't send American prunes back to America.'

'You promised to help us.'

'Yes, I am willing to help. The US post office doesn't care if I send clothes, but food is prohibited. The US government is sending food to starving Europeans and you want me to send a heavy parcel of prunes back to the States?'

'You can't do this as a favour?'

'Sorry. Clothes, yes; prunes, no.'

My refusal meant the cooling of our friendship.

* * *

I visited the Jewish Displaced Persons (DP) camp in Zeilsheim near Hoechst. It was situated on a housing estate. There were about 40 detached houses each with a little garden, housing several hundred liberated Jews. The commander of the camp was David Schonberg of the American Joint Distribution Committee. He was a broad-shouldered, genial-looking man. He told me: 'It's a hard job, believe me. They don't appreciate what I'm doing. They blame me for things that I can't change. The other day when I arrived in the morning, my office was plastered with swastikas.'

'That's terrible,' I said, horrified.

'Yes, it is.'

'Did you find out who did it?'

'No, the camp people knew all right, but wouldn't say.'

I talked to the DP leader. He said: 'The trouble with Schonberg is he can't talk directly to us. He doesn't speak Polish, Yiddish or German. So we can only talk through an interpreter. We hate the food we get.'

'What's wrong with it?'

'It's all tins. Only tinned food. No fresh vegetables.'

'Why don't you grow your own vegetables? There's plenty of ground around these houses.' I pointed to the large gardens surrounding each house. They were all overgrown with weeds.

He seemed to be annoyed by my remark. 'That's what Schonberg says. We will never grow anything on German soil. We want to get out. We've been waiting now for nearly a year.'

'Where do you want to go to?'

'Eretz Israel of course. The British won't let us in. But some of us have succeeded.'

'How?'

'Well, I'll tell you how we do it because you're a Jew. The Jewish Brigade which is stationed in Italy has organized a courier service to Holland. On the way back from Holland they give us forged papers. We just go with them and then off to Palestine.'

'How many of you go every week?'

'That depends on how many forged papers we get. It's about 12 people – not enough, of course.'

* * *

Genuine anti-Nazis in Frankfurt were a tiny minority. I visited the office dealing with German political concentration camp survivors in Frankfurt. The office was small and shabby looking. It was partly bomb damaged, like so many buildings in the city. A crack in the wall looked ominous, as though it might collapse soon. The place looked empty – there was hardly any furniture. Its chairman Herr Roth, himself a survivor, was tall, bespectacled and had a slight limp. He said:

'We believe the entire German people is guilty of having supported Hitler. They are also guilty of the Nazis' crimes. Yes, everyone of us. I accuse myself too for not having done enough to overthrow Hitler.'

Herr Roth was one of several thousand political prisoners liberated from Buchenwald concentration camp. In Frankfurt there were 1,500 residents who had been liberated from these camps. Two-thirds of them were non-Jewish and were political prisoners. Those who belonged to political parties were mostly communists and social democrats. Roth continued:

'Now, party allegiance matters little. The main problem is re-education and de-Nazification. Too many Nazis are again in high positions and are flouting the de-Nazification law under the very nose of the US military government. Meanwhile our personal well-being is neglected. On arrival from the camps everybody received 300 Marks. We were

Hermann Blumenthal 80 Jahre.

Blumenthal seinen achtzigsten Geburtstag. Geboren am 28. April 1849 besuchte er das Realgymnasium in Bromberg und absolvierte seine Lehrzeit bei einer Eisengroßhandlung. Er genügte dann seiner Militärzeit und gehört zu den wenigen lebenden Veteranen aus dem Kriege 1870/71, die die Schlacht von Sedan mitgemacht

haben. Er gründete dann am 1. Mai 1874 eine Kohlen- und Baustoffhandlung in Bromberg, so daß die Firma auf ein 55 jähriges Bestehen zurücksehen kann. Herr Blumenthal selbst dürfte wohl mit zu den ältesten Kohlen- und Baustoffhändlern gehören. Die Firma verlegte dann vor 20 Jahren ihr Hauptgeschäft nach Berlin, während in Bromberg eine Zweigniederlassung verblieb. Im Jahre 1918 schloß die Firma sich dem Konzern der Kokswerke und Chemischen Fabriken A.-G. an. Die Firma und ihre Leiter erfreuen sich im Kreise ihrer Fachgenossen und weit darüber hinaus größter Wertschätzung.

1. The coal trade journal, *Deutsche Kohlenzeitung*, congratulates grandfather Blumenthal on his eightieth birthday. It mentions that he was one of the survivors of the 1870–71 Franco-Prussian War and that he took part in the battle of Sedan.

2. Mutti in Bromberg, where she was born: 'the prettiest girl in town.'

3. Detta Emma and me.

4. Mutti (on the left), with Vati, an unnamed
   friend, and me in the Grunewald.

6. Bruder Hans, me, Patschke and son Rainer, at
   the Wannsee.

5. Onkel Benno and me.

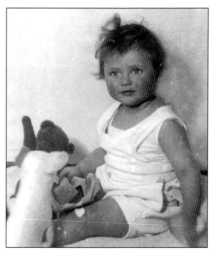

7. Me and my teddy bears.

8. Vati's firm. The letter heading reads: 'Founded in 1821. Gold Medal Berlin 1907. Supplier to His Majesty the Emperor and King. Suitcase Manufacturer. Factory for Travel Goods. Wholesale and Export and Army Equipment. Own Carpentry and Locksmith. Supplier to various authorities, including the Colonial Office, and the Detachment of the Imperial Guard.'

9. Bobby Feistmann and me on our first day at school, 1929.

10. Onkel Franz and Mutti.

11. Even at the age of eight years, I showed political awareness. The underlined section of my essay reads: 'Hitler has won the provincial elections. On Sunday I travelled to Vati by overhead railway (because it is too dangerous to go by bus) and the soldiers marched without music so that we had to return home without having seen anything. The police carry rifles.'

12. Onkel Domke and Detta Emma in their 'house on the hill' in Caminchen;
    my happiest time in Germany.

13. Luz and me in Werder practising target shooting.

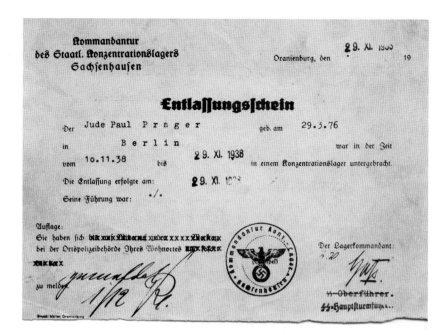

14. Vati's certificate of release from Sachsenhausen.

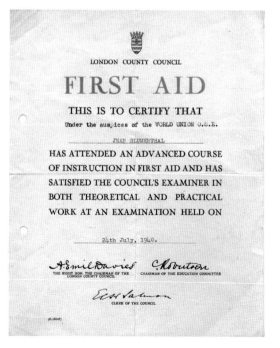

15. Onkel Jean was declared proficient in First Aid (after 20 years of successful practice in Berlin). His title of 'Doctor' was omitted, as his degree was not recognised in the UK.

16. Bruder Hans, Gretel, and children.

17. Phillip Woolley, the Oxford graduate who stood outside the Goldschmidtschule with a stick warding off the Hitler Youth. He became temporary Head of the school. Picture taken at the Berlin reunion in 1992.

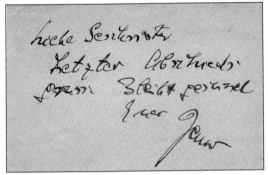

18. Onkel Benno's last postcard, written to Mutti and Onkel Franz on the day of his deportation. 'Dear brother and sister, last farewell. Keep well. Yours Benno.'

19. The plaque at the Grunewald Gymnasium, now called the Walther Rathenau Schule. A Ginko tree has been planted in the playground in memory of the Jewish pupils who fell victim to the Nazis.

20. Me in Berlin while working in the US Civil Censorship Division.

21. *'Gebt uns unsere Männer wieder'* ('Return our husbands to us'): a sculpture in the Rosenstrasse to commemorate the 2,000 gentile women who successfully demonstrated outside the Rosenstrasse prison where their Jewish husbands were waiting to be sent to Auschwitz.

22. Reunion of former classmates from the Grunewald Gymnasium, at the East German Baltic seaside resort of Ahrenshoop, September 2001. Peter Prager, first row, second left, with Sylvia on his left.

given ration cards for almost everything, but we still have the coupons because the goods are unobtainable.'

After the interview Mr Roth led me to a backroom where the pleasant smell of fresh butter greeted me.

'A present from the Americans, I presume?' I asked.

'No,' he said bitterly, 'this is a present from a Swiss charity. The Americans will not give us anything because we are Germans.'

Justice

I carried on with my job as postal censor. We were supposed to find black marketeers and war criminals, and to report what Germans thought of the various occupying forces.

In 1946 the guards of Belsen concentration camp were tried. The main defendant was Kramer, the camp commandant who was known as the Beast of Belsen. He was found guilty and executed. One day among the letters I censored I came across a letter from a girlfriend of Kramer's daughter: 'During the last few days I have read terrible things about your father. I have often visited your home and I know your parents' Christian way of life. I want to assure you that I shall never believe the things that the newspapers say your father was supposed to have done.'

Similarly, Hoess, the commandant of Auschwitz, declared in his autobiography that he could not hate Jews, for hatred was alien to his character. He was a family man and an animal lover, and every day he looked forward to coming home to his wife and three children, from whom he kept secret his daytime activities. He did not like his job, but it was not his business to question the wisdom of orders from Himmler. During the trial he did not try to excuse himself, nor his deeds. He told an uncomprehending court: *'Befehl ist Befehl! –* A command is a command!'

On another occasion I intercepted a letter sent by Manfred, the 17-year-old son of Fieldmarshal Rommel. Later Manfred became Mayor of Stuttgart. The letter contained a sworn statement before a magistrate on the true facts about his father's death. If the 20 July plot had succeeded, Rommel, who was one of the conspirators, would have become president of the new Germany. The statement said: 'My father was expecting arrest. The Gestapo arrived. They said to him, "This is your choice. We have orders to take you to Berlin. You will be tried for high treason and will certainly be found guilty. You will be executed and your family will be put into a concentration camp. Your other choice is to shoot yourself, and your family will be spared. Here is a revolver." My father said goodbye and left by car. We didn't see him again.' The following day the radio announced: 'Fieldmarshal Rommel has been killed in an air raid. The Führer has ordered a state funeral.'

Coming Home

I regularly visited a group of students from Frankfurt University who had been demobilized from the German army. On one visit I found them all sitting dejectedly. I asked them what was the matter.

'Have you read Baldur von Schirach's statement at Nürnberg?' they asked.

'I have. He didn't divulge anything we didn't know already,' I answered.

'He did,' they said. 'It was he above everyone else who made us believe that our cause was just and noble. We believed him. Our faith in Hitler has already been broken, but his confession has utterly shattered us. We fought and endured this terrible war and the man who told us to die for our country has admitted he misled us.'

Here is Baldur von Schirach's confession as spoken on 24 May 1946 at the War Crimes Trial in Nürnberg.

I have educated this generation in faith and loyalty to Hitler. The youth organization which I built up bore his name. I believed that I was serving a leader who would make our people and the youth of our country great and happy and free. Millions of young people believed this, together with me, and saw their ultimate ideal in National Socialism. Many died for it. Before God, before the German nation, and before my German people I alone bear the guilt of having trained our young people for a man whom I for many long years had considered unimpeachable, both as a leader and as the head of State, in creating for him a generation who saw him as I did. The guilt is mine in that I educated the youth of Germany for a man who murdered by the million. I believed in this man, that is all I can say for my excuse and for the characterization of my attitude. This is my own personal guilt. I was responsible for the youth of the country. I was placed in authority over the young people, and the guilt is mine alone.

Hitler is dead. I never betrayed him; I never tried to overthrow him; I remained true to my oath as an officer, a youth leader, and an official. I was no blind collaborator of his; neither was I an opportunist. I was a convinced National Socialist from my earliest days – as such, I was also an anti-Semite. Hitler's racial policy was a crime which led to the disaster of 5,000,000 Jews and for all Germans. The younger generation bears no guilt. But he who after Auschwitz, still clings to racial politics has rendered himself guilty.

I thought back to the times of the Grunewald Gymnasium, when my classmates had been enthused by the new era which the Hitler Youth had promised. These young men in Frankfurt had, no doubt, been equally gripped by the chauvinist fervour which had developed in Germany at the time. Now they had come to grips with the truth.

19 Reunion with Mutti

As soon as I had arrived in Offenbach I made an application to my commanding officer. I asked to be granted compassionate leave to go to Berlin to see my mother. I explained that I had not seen her for six years.

The next day I was called to the CO's office. His adjutant saw me: 'You've just arrived and immediately ask for leave. You're here to do a job. To get to Berlin you have to cross the Russian Zone. Therefore no leave is granted. Application rejected.'

I decided to go without permission.

* * *

The nearest stop on the route before the Russian Zone was Kassel. I applied for a weekend pass to Kassel. It was granted for New Year's Eve 1945. I started my preparations. It was no use taking money to Mutti, as it had lost its value. Cigarettes were the thing. My ration was 200 cigarettes and 20 cigars per week, and I didn't smoke. One cigarette was worth 10 Marks, making me rich. I decided to collect as many weeks' supplies as possible and get everything useful from the PX: candy, peanuts, fruit juice and soap.

On 31 December I left for the station. The cases were so heavy that I could only drag them along the ground, but I had to pretend that I only carried personal belongings as US personnel caught black marketeering could be heavily punished. Everybody on the train was going to Berlin. I only had a weekend pass to Kassel, several hundred miles from Berlin.

'Why these heavy cases just for a weekend?' The Military Policeman looked at me and my papers.

I knew I'd be done for if he looked inside my cases. Tense moments passed.

'Go on,' he said. Perhaps he was slightly drunk. After all it was New Year's Eve.

But the danger was not yet over: there was bound to be another check when the train got moving. I had to be on the lookout all the time. I found a seat and put the cases on the luggage rack. I was exhausted. The train started and I slept.

* * *

The compartment door opens. A sinister figure enters. I crouch into the corner. The sinister figure walks straight towards me. I am half lying, half sitting and I shiver all over. I am very frightened. I wish something terrible would happen – sudden lightening, thunder, or an explosion which would shake the entire train, perhaps a crash creating confusion would drive this sinister figure away from me. He opens his horrible mouth. His white teeth are shining. God, will you not help me? This monster. His words will eat me up. I know they will. I put my fingers into both ears. I can still hear him. He shouts. I am ready for the worst.

'This is the Military Police! We want to check your travel orders. What do you mean, Kassel. Right in the Russian Zone? We'll dump you there! Corporal, arrest this man! He is AWOL. We are looking for guys like you. Follow the corporal. If he resists take him by force!'

I feel sweat running down my face. My heart beats heavily. I tremble all over. I won't follow the corporal. I can't follow him. I must not go!

* * *

I open my eyes. A GI train guard with a pistol round his belt stands grinning in front of me and is about to shake me.

'Hey, fellow, what's the matter with you? Don't you want any breakfast? What's all this sweat round your face? Had a nightmare? Well, no wonder in these lousy trains. Either you can't sleep or you have bad dreams. All of you ought to have sleepers. Poor fellows. Sleepers for officers only. Who won the war anyway? Hurry up. Chow's ready. Eggs for breakfast.' He disappears. I take my handkerchief out of my pocket and wipe my face.

The others have already hurried to the dining car. I look out of the window. We have just entered the Province of Brandenburg. Not far to go. I put on my tie, comb my hair and go for breakfast. A young blonde sits opposite me.

'Good morning, wasn't it a comfortable night? I adore sleepers. Don't you? How did you sleep?'

I look at her. She is really pretty. What a shame I have to meet her just now. My mind isn't on girls. 'Yes, the journey was comfortable,' I reply.

We pass slowly through a town, Brandenburg/Havel.

'Is Havel a big town?' the blonde asks. 'No, Havel is a river, Brandenburg is the town,' I answer.

'You seem to know this area.'

I finish my two eggs and coffee and leave before she can ask any more questions.

We reached Potsdam, where the station was terribly bombed. There was a direct hit on the railway depot. The blast had lifted one engine on top of another, while another was still, after nearly a year, lying upside-down. The scene looked like the aftermath of a battle between monsters.

Only a few more minutes to go. I had never felt so excited in all my life. The last time I cried openly was when I was 15 and kissed my mother goodbye, not knowing whether I would ever see her again. The few tears I shed in the year I arrived in England I suppressed because I believed that only women cry, not men. There was a certain beauty in crying women, men could fall in love with them, women would never fall in love with crying men. And yet, at the moment, I felt I would soon burst into tears, tears of joy.

My compartment filled again with smoking, half-sleeping GIs. Neubabelsberg, the Ufa film studios. The place was full of red flags and a huge picture of Stalin could be seen in the market square. Another five minutes and the train rolled into Wannsee, the terminus for US military trains. I got out but had difficulties with my two heavy cases. A porter came up to me: 'Can I help?' He spoke the Berlin dialect, the first time I had heard it since I left in 1938. He helped me to the local train. From Wannsee it was another 10 minutes to Charlottenburg station. I used to wait there every day for Onkel Franz to return from work. While waiting I watched the rabbits burrowing in the railway embankment.

* * *

I am so near. I cart the cases towards Nieburstrasse, I hardly feel their weight. I pass the ruins of the building which used to be our butcher's. I loathed buying meat; I never knew the difference between pork, lamb or beef. Then my mother would send me back with an angry note and the butcher would tell me off for having asked for the wrong things. Is he still alive? I pass the dairy which delivered our milk and rolls every morning. Just before I left, the milkman's son had arranged his first window display. The father was proud. We all congratulated him on the excellent display. Later Mutti told me he was missing in Russia.

Number 58. The front of the building is completely destroyed, but we lived at the back courtyard on the third floor which, by a miracle, is untouched. I don't know how I carry my two cases up three flights of stairs. Will Mutti be at home? Because I had been refused permission to come, I could not tell her that I am on the way. I ring the bell.

'Who is there?' she asks.

'It's me.'

Mutti opens the door. 'My boy, my boy,' she cries, and we fall into each other's arms. 'I have you back at last!' I am crying.

She looks frail and old. Onkel Franz is haggard and thin; he will soon succumb to his last illness. We talk and talk. She names people who had helped them through those terrible times, and also those who didn't. The last days of Onkel Paul and Tante Lotte and Onkel Benno were spent in Mutti's flat before their deportation. And Onkel Richard and Tante Else had survived, being hidden by Christians for two and a half years.

Mutti told how Tante Emma was taken by train from Theresienstadt concentration camp to Switzerland thanks to an SS general who bargained for his life in exchange for a trainload of Jews. How Tante Cläre and Onkel Georg were transported to Theresienstadt. Onkel Georg, a diabetic, died on the journey. Tante Cläre never came back. How my schoolfriend Hans Goldman visited Mutti regularly until he was deported and was never heard of again.

I slept that night in my old room. I thought back to 1938 when I had last slept in my bed. How had my feelings changed since then? As a 15-year-old my thoughts were conditioned by my mother. Whenever I thought ahead, I tried to imagine what she would want me to do and then I'd make my plans accordingly. It was different now. I considered it my duty to help my mother and Onkel Franz in every possible way, but my future plans were my own. I would inform them, after I had decided for myself. The idea of letting them decide my future did not occur to me. I was responsible for my own fate.

The next day Hans, who was stationed in Berlin, took me on a sightseeing trip by jeep through the inner city. I had experienced devastated towns, but what I saw now appalled me. Miles and miles of rubble as far as the eye could see. The roads had been cleared for traffic. Otherwise ruins and ruins. Hans would call out: 'Alexander Platz, Unter den Linden, Monbijou Platz.' I recognized nothing.

The weekend went quickly. Boarding the train on my way back presented a more difficult problem. Going to Berlin I could board the train officially because Kassel was on the way. If I showed my pass now I would be apprehended immediately. The MPs were checking everybody as they boarded the train. I stood there with my two cases which, happily, were quite light. I decided to walk on to the other side and get on to the train from the track. A few Germans saw me but they did not care. I found a seat. As soon as we started the MPs began to check everybody's pass. There was no way out. I braced myself for the worst. The MP looked at my papers.

'How did you get to Berlin?'

'I just boarded the train at Frankfurt.'

'Come with me.' He took me to the train commander.

'These are all the papers he's got.' The MP showed the train commander my pass to Kassel.

'You are under arrest!' Then he turned to the MP. 'Stop the train! Throw him out. He can walk to Frankfurt.'

Did he mean it? Surely not. If somebody in US army

uniform is seen walking about in the Russian Zone, this would be an international incident. But perhaps he did mean it. I wasn't sure. For a few seconds I felt quite faint. Then I noticed that the MP was still standing behind me. He was supposed to stop the train. I saw a twinkle in the train commander's eye. 'I'll send a report to your Provost Marshal. If this happens again I will throw you off the train. Go back to your seat.' I was saved.

The following day I was called before the Provost Marshal. 'What did you do in Berlin?'

'I saw my mother for the first time since the war.'

'Your mother?' He seemed surprised.

'Yes, Captain.'

He looked at me for some seconds. 'Don't do it again.' He dismissed me. There were no repercussions.

20   Berlin during the War

Mutti was one of the few Jews who lived in Berlin throughout the war. She tells me what happened.

'It is 1943. The Nazi warden tells us that we are not allowed to use the communal air-raid shelter, so Onkel Franz and I install ourselves in our own cellar. After the next air raid the warden comes to us and says: "As none of the others object to you, you can stay with us after all." Onkel Franz replies: "Thank you very much, but we're quite comfortable where we are."

'During one of the air raids the cry goes through the building: "the roof is on fire!" Onkel Franz and all the other men rush to the top and extinguish the flames. A napalm bomb sprays Onkel Franz's hand.'

'Did it hurt a lot?'

'Napalm only burns when exposed to air. He covered his hand and held it tight to prevent air touching it. This was a very heavy raid in which thousands were killed. The next morning he tried to get first aid but couldn't. He's told, "stretcher cases only". We decided he had to go to his mother in the country. There was no public transport, so he walked with his covered hand for two hours through burning Berlin until he reached Anhalter Bahnhof. He caught a train to Zeitz, where he was treated, then he came back to me.

'Some time later a rumour went round: "Jewish wives of Aryan husbands will be arrested." I packed all my valuables and gave them to Fräulein Rossdorf. Do you remember her?'

'Yes, of course. She lives next door doesn't she?'

'That's right. When I handed them to her she burst out crying: "I'm ashamed to be a German." Dr Epping who is an anti-Nazi gave me a poison phial: "When you can't stand it, swallow it and in a few minutes you'll be dead." As you know I can only walk with a stick. I couldn't go on any march.

Finally the Gestapo did arrest me and took me to the Gestapo headquarter in Albrecht Strasse. Onkel Franz brought me food parcels every day but I didn't get them. Then, after two weeks I was released. No explanation was given. But Onkel Franz was arrested instead. I've already told you what happened to him.'

'Did you know what went on at Auschwitz?'

'Yes, unfortunately I did.'

'How?'

'You remember Frau Sinn?'

'Of course I do. She was the last cleaning lady.'

'She is a good sort. When the Russians arrested her husband because he was a Nazi Party member, she remarked: "I cannot really complain considering what you and your family have gone through." Well, her husband worked on the railways. His mate was an engine driver who took transports to Auschwitz. He told her husband and she told me. She knew I wouldn't denounce her for it was considered treason to tell anybody the truth about the gas chambers. I vomited when I heard it and couldn't eat for a whole day. Soon after, Onkel Paul, Tante Lotte and Onkel Benno got their notices for deportation. I decided not to tell them. What was the use? They were not like Onkel Richard and Tante Else who had somewhere to hide. They had nowhere to go and Tante Lotte was sure she would come back after the war. The day they left I was in a terrible state. Just on that day Albert paid a visit.'

'The manager of the coal mine near Leipzig?'

'Yes, him. The one who brought you the fossils before the war.'

'I remember.'

'Well, he saw me in this terrible state and he tried to cheer me up. He said, "Don't worry. All your family will return after the war. They've been sent east to escape the bombing." You know he's always sympathized with the Nazis and I had the impression that he actually believed what he said.'

* * *

'Now it is spring 1945. The final days of the war. A shell had killed the Nazi warden. We didn't shed a tear. When we heard artillery fire we all went to our cellar. There was no food but a dead horse was lying just outside our house. This provided our only food for several days.

'Suddenly the shooting stops. A brave boy crawls out of the cellar. He reports: "Our troops have gone. The Russians must arrive any minute." The first tank appears. From all corners people are looking to see what he will do. A soldier opens the hatch and throws something into the street. A boy runs forward to pick it up. "It's bread," he shouts. The people of Niebuhrstrasse run into the street. Other tanks arrive. Bread, biscuits, chocolates and cigarettes are thrown to the people.

'There is an announcement through a loudspeaker: "We need to be put up for the night. We ask you to open your homes to us."

'A very young soldier is billeted with me. He looked like you. I tried to explain this to him but he didn't understand. He asked for a pen and paper. I suppose he wanted to write home. He slept in your room in your bed. The next day he moved on with the other fighting soldiers. The occupation army moved in. Things changed. Houses were plundered, women raped. Do you remember Tatjana from the first floor?'

'She was a White Russian.'

'Yes, she was a Nazi and an anti-Semite. We intended to tell the Red Army. But she spoke Russian. She prevented our house from being ransacked and none of us was raped. She became our saviour. She still lives here. Though we are now in the British Sector we dare not denounce her in case the Russians come back.'

As Mutti tells me her story the bell rings. It is Frau Melcynski, Mutti's cleaner from a long time ago. I remembered that this enthusiastic Nazi wanted me on 1 May 1935 to march to the Lustgarten to cheer the Führer. Now she fell into Mutti's arms.

'I'm so glad to see you after all these years.'

'A pity you never came when we needed you,' Mutti replied.

'But all you had to do was to ask me. I never agreed with the Nazis' anti-Semitism. And you never asked for help.'

'What do you want?' Mutti replied curtly.

'Well, you see, when I cleaned your place, I of course knew

you were Jewish but I didn't mind. I worked for you to show my opposition to the Nazis. I want you to put this in a statement for the occupying powers. I want to be de-Nazified.'

* * *

I was working in the main Berlin communication centre. All telephone cables ran through this building: cables from Moscow to the Red Army headquarters in Karlshorst, from the US Headquarters, Frankfurt to the US Kommandantura in Berlin, and of course the British and the French. Each occupying power used a separate floor. Officially our work consisted of monitoring German civilian telephone conversations, but the American and British listened to the Russians while the Russians did the same with the Americans and British.

We had lunch at the Allied Kommandantura where I rubbed shoulders with all allied personnel. When sitting with Red Army soldiers it was very difficult to talk to them. It wasn't the language problem – the Russians spoke excellent German – but they had instructions not to talk to Western soldiers. On one occasion I was able to start a conversation with three Red Army women officers.

'It is remarkable how quickly the theatres rose out of the ruins,' I said.

'Yes, they are of a very high standard,' they replied. 'Because of the food shortage we allow the actors to eat at our officers' mess.'

'That must be the reason why they are able to act so well.' After dinner I said: 'Have an American cigarette.' Immediately they got up and left, looking disgusted. They had been told: 'If an American offers you cigarettes, refuse, because it is an indecent suggestion.'

21   Onkel Richard

'Peter, can you come tomorrow after school to play soldiers?'

'Alright, I'll be there.' I loved going to my cousin Luz because Onkel Richard and Tante Else always served such lovely suppers which my parents could never afford: smoked salmon, strawberry gâteau with whipped cream, and you could eat as much as you liked. Onkel Richard and Tante Else Gelhar were my mother's cousins. Onkel Richard had grown rich by trading in sugar, and was a millionaire. He was short, thick-set, blue eyed, grey haired, and had a jolly outgoing manner. Tante Else was short and plump with black hair and blue eyes, and was always talking. They were the only people in my family who were religious. They kept all the Jewish holidays and Friday night was always their special night with candles, prayers and chollah (called *barches* in German).

They lived in a flat in Schmargendorf opposite my school. Their son, Luz, was my age. We played toy-soldiers and, like most German boys at the time, this was our favourite game. We shot each other's soldiers with wooden pellets and the one who was able to kill most had won the game.

The Gelhars had a weekend villa in Werder, a small town near Potsdam along the River Havel. Onkel Richard had land there on which he built a house. There was a landing stage along its private beach where his motor yacht was moored. Every few weeks Tante Else phoned to ask if I wanted to go with them for the weekend. I always said yes; I enjoyed these weekends.

On Sundays before breakfast I fished from the landing stage. After breakfast Onkel Richard would take us out on the river in his boat. Before lunch I swam to the island in the middle of the lake. In the evening my uncle motored back to Berlin. It was a luxury weekend, never quite real to me because everything I experienced there was beyond my parents' reach. It was like fairyland. The last time I stayed there was August 1938.

* * *

On 9 November came Kristallnacht. To escape arrest my uncle and aunt fled to Werder, hoping the Gestapo would not find out. In the middle of their first night there, they were woken up by a thunderous noise. Nobody had rung the bell. They looked out of the window. Stormtroopers were hacking down the front door with an axe and they broke into the house. Onkel Richard recounted:

'They were like wild beasts. Their eyes were starting from their heads and they were drunk. They screamed and swung their axes over their heads like Red Indians on the warpath. We fled in our nightclothes to the lake and waited. We heard the smashing of windows and the crash of furniture thrown into the garden.

'At dawn it quietened down and we returned. We found a scene of unbelievable destruction. The stormtroopers had gone about axing everything they could find – furniture, crockery, pictures, gramophone records. All the doors had been broken down, and in their fury they even tried to tear apart towels, clothes and bedsheets. We left Werder never to return.'

All of us were filled with great despondency, but Onkel Richard behaved as though he knew exactly what to do. He recounted the events in Werder as though they were an outrage to be fought against, rather than the beginning of the end. Onkel Franz said that Onkel Richard had something up his sleeve. What was it? American friends had sent him an affidavit to emigrate there, but quota restrictions meant he would have to wait four years. Then it would be too late. Meanwhile Luz succeeded in emigrating to Palestine. What were Onkel Richard's plans? I found out when I returned to Berlin as a soldier in 1945.

Mass deportation of Jews to Poland began in 1941, under the official cover of 'resettlement'. Neither Germans nor Jews were told anything about extermination and, as hope is eternal, many Jews hoped they would somehow survive the war.

* * *

In 1945 Onkel Richard recounted to me: 'I didn't know what was going to happen to us in Poland and I didn't intend to find out. No resettlement for me. The authorities told us several days in advance when and where we should assemble for the transport. One day in May 1942 I received the following letter:

The Jewish Community
Berlin N. 4
29 May 1942

Concerns Migration
The authorities have ordered your migration for 2 June 1942. This applies to your wife and any single member of your family if they have submitted a property statement. Should they have received a notification for postponement, this notification should be returned with all relevant particulars to the Jewish Community.

On Sunday 31 May you can deposit your luggage between 09.00–13.00 hours at the collection point Levetzostrasse 7/8. On Monday 1 June at 06.00 hours officials will seal your flat. You have to be ready at that time to hand over the keys to the officials.

We are responsible for catering arrangements at the collection point and during the journey. However, you should bring with your hand luggage any leftover food, and in particular sandwiches.

At the collection point and during the journey social workers and carers will be in attendance. All necessary medicines will be handed out solely by First Aid personnel.

Enclosed you will find a notice giving all directions to be followed. We earnestly ask you to follow these directions and to prepare for the transport in a calm and level-headed way. You must realize that by your personal example in carrying out all instructions you will be able to contribute to the smooth running of the transport. Naturally we shall, as far as it is permitted, assist our members and render all possible assistance.

The Executive of the Jewish Community in Berlin

Onkel Richard carried on: 'On Sunday 31 May Else and I packed our suitcases and left very early in the morning pretending to go to the assembly point, but the authorities never saw us again. Months earlier we'd made arrangements to stay with Hans Schmidt, our former chauffeur. Among the neighbours and friends we passed for a bombed-out uncle and aunt.'

'You must have had some hair raising escapes,' I said.

'Oh yes we did. I'll tell you of one: One evening we were sitting together with some friends of Schmidt. They wanted to meet us. Else, who is inclined to be a bit boastful, mentioned that we used to have a season ticket for the Deutsche Theater. The next day one of the friends said to Hans: "No relations of yours have ever gone to the Deutsche Theater. They are Jews." You can imagine how frightened we all were that he'd tell the Gestapo. According to Nazi law, you were guilty of high treason if you knew of a Jew in hiding and didn't report it. Well, he didn't.

'That was a bit of luck wasn't it?' I said.

'Yes, it was. But Schmidt's friends hated Nazis just as much as Schmidt hated them. I'll tell you another story: I was cycling along trying to get some black market food when I was stopped by a military policeman. 'Papers please!' he shouted.

'"I left them at home," I said.

'"I'm afraid, you'll have to come with me for identification."

'If I had done this it would have been the end of me. I searched my pockets and found an envelope addressed to Hans Schmidt. "I'm Hans Schmidt. Here is an envelope to prove it."

'The military policeman looked at the envelope and at me. Perhaps I looked honest or perhaps he was keen to come off duty. He just said: "All right, you can go. Next time don't come out without papers."

'It took me a while to recuperate from this fright. We all decided that Else and I must get some identity papers. Hans knew a policeman who often expressed anti-Nazi views. He was approached and he said he'd give us temporary papers with an address of a recently bombed house. He told us to come back in three months and he'd give me and Else papers from a different address. Then Hans himself was bombed out.

'We had made provisions for this and moved to Herman Braun, another Gentile home. There must have been perhaps 20 people who protected us from certain death. You know, 1,500 Jews emerged from hiding after liberation – not many considering there were 150,000 Jews in Berlin before – but this means that at least 30,000 Berliners risked their lives for us.'

* * *

'In the spring of 1945, the Red Army fought its way into Berlin. We heard artillery fire approaching our district and waited in communal street shelters. People were terrified of what the approaching Russians would do to them. One of the occupants said to me: "If only we had a Jew among us, he would be able to save our lives."

'"Yes," I said. "You're quite right, but it's a bit late to think of it now." Then the Russians came.

'A notice was plastered on every street corner. Everyone must hand in all weapons within 24 hours. Anybody who fails to do so will be shot.'

Many Germans were afraid to do this, lest they were accused of being terrorists but they were also frightened to keep their weapons, so they threw them into other people's property. A couple of rifles landed in our garden. Suddenly a Red Army soldier approached us.

'"Who's the owner of this house?"

'"I am," said Braun.

'"You've not obeyed orders. We found these rifles in your garden."

'"They're not mine."

'"We're not interested in excuses. You'll be shot."

'Braun protested: "We've been hiding Jews and have always been anti-Nazi."

'The officer laughed. "Every German we meet says that he's been anti-Nazi and helped Jews."

'I stepped forward and explained who I was.

'"Give us proof. Where are your papers?" Years earlier all relevant documents had been buried in the garden, but where exactly? The officer gave us two hours to find them.

'"Let's dig!' shouts Herman. We all dig like mad. Meanwhile the Red Army soldiers make leisurely preparations for the execution. Else hits something solid. We rush to her. It's the box. It contains Else's and my passport, marked J for Jew, our deportation orders and all documents proving our antecedents.

"Here you are." We show them to the soldiers. They are amazed. An interpreter was called who was also a Jew. "Shalom," he said to me.

'"Shalom," I answered. Suddenly we, together with our saviours, became heroes. The Russians brought us food, cigarettes and all kinds of presents, and to show their appreciation, they decided to establish brigade headquarters in our house. They explained: "You can all carry on living here in the upstairs rooms and you'll have plenty of food because you'll eat with us." This was a remarkable concession, for at the time the German population was starving.

'Afterwards I was able to recover my villa in Dahlem, which the Nazis had confiscated and which is in the American zone. We decided to move there.'

'Is this the villa?'

'Yes, it is. We're sitting in it now. As you know it is in the American officers' compound. I received special permission to live here.'

* * *

I visited Onkel Richard regularly. He soon became the centre of intense commercial activity, overwhelmed by American cigarettes which he sold to the Germans on the black market. At the time money was valueless and everyone traded in cigarettes. They were too valuable to smoke and ordinary financial transactions were conducted on the basis of, say, 100 Marks plus 15 cigarettes. Onkel Richard prospered on this.

I was then a telephone censor in the US Army. We were given watchlists of suspicious people, whose phone conversations were to be recorded on tape day and night. One day I was given a new list and I found the following: 'Gelhar, Richard. Suspected of black market dealings with US Army personnel.' That was me! I didn't know what to do. I couldn't tell him as he would stop telephoning and that would cast suspicion on me. I could be court-martialled. This had actually happened to a friend of mine.

Next time I went to see him I remarked casually, 'Is it wise to make illegal deals over the phone?'

He looked straight at me and asked: 'Why? Does anybody suspect me?'

'Oh, I was just wondering,' I replied.

'Listen,' he said. 'The Gestapo didn't catch me and the Americans aren't going to catch me either.'

The following week I received a phone call at my flat. 'When you come tomorrow could you bring 100 packets of "C"?'

'I don't know,' I replied, and rang off.

When I saw him, I said: 'You know, you frightened the life out of me with your phone call.'

He replied: 'To please you, I especially said "C" instead of cigarettes. Anyway, is there a telephone censorship?' I said nothing and changed the subject.

When he applied for a US visa Onkel Richard was given a stiff interview by the American consul. Somehow he satisfied the consul about how he made his living and he received a visa.

On his journey to America his entire luggage was stolen. He had not insured it because he didn't have enough dollars, but he was not dismayed. He became an antique dealer – a new profession for him – and soon became prosperous again. When he was 80, Aunt Else died. Six months later Onkel Richard married again. 'Life must go on,' he wrote.

Nothing could have been more characteristic.

To me Onkel Richard was the greatest hero in my whole family, except for Onkel Franz. He never let circumstances get him down. He never allowed himself to be overcome by suffering. He took the bull by the horns – and won.

22 Family Müller-Siemens

When Mutti divorced Vati in 1929, he moved to the boarding house run by Family Müller-Siemens at Monbijou Platz in the centre of Berlin. It was the same place in which he had stayed before he married. His marriage in pieces, his business in ruins, at 51 he had reached the nadir of his life.

Frau Müller-Siemens was a tall, stout woman with a commanding air. She was a descendant of the famous Siemens family, hence the double-barrelled name. Herr Müller was blind in one eye because of a painting accident while decorating his flat. He was short with black hair. He had a sweet shop but could not make ends meet, so his wife kept a boarding house with a number of permanent guests. Vati was one of them, and it was there I visited him every weekend.

The Müllers, like millions of Germans, were attracted to National Socialism because the Nazis had promised to lift them out of the depression. Herr Müller joined the party in 1932, one year before their ascent to power. He explained why he kept his friendship with Vati: 'You see, he's a decent chap. I know him personally. He's an exception.'

Vati was treated like one of the family by the Müllers and so was I.

'Peter, I have brought you something from the shop,' Herr Müller said when I arrived on a Saturday.

'Thank you very much. Marzipan is my favourite.'

Annelies, their daughter, and I became great friends. We used to dress up and give the adults a surprise by putting on little plays for them. I was looking forward all week to seeing Annelies and showing off while the adults had their coffee and cakes. Herr and Frau Müller, Vati and the lodgers watched us and, like the children, enjoyed these afternoons. To me they were bliss.

One day Herr Müller said to Vati: 'We're behind with the

rent and we've been given notice. We must look for cheaper premises.'

'What am I going to do when you move?' Vati asked.

'Don't worry Herr Prager. You're one of the family. You will move with us of course.' The cheaper premises were in Siegmundshof, Tiergarten. They took Vati with them, even though he could not pay anything as his firm had gone bankrupt. The pension was situated opposite the Adass Jisroel School, an Orthodox Jewish school, and from Vati's room on the fourth floor I watched the boys with their yarmulkes on their heads going into the small school synagogue. As I had not been brought up in a religious home, the boys looked strange to me. We were fellow Jews but I could not identify with them.

At the pension, politics were never discussed. One day Müller announced: 'I've decided to change my daily paper from the *Lokal Anzeiger* [rightwing] to the *Völkischer Beobachter* [Nazi]. I'm also joining the SA [stormtroopers]. They want to promote me to officer and I swore an oath of allegiance to Hitler. During the First World War I had sworn a similar oath to the Kaiser. I can't swear allegiance to two people.'

'But this oath is invalid because of the Kaiser's abdication,' Vati said.

'Oh no. I don't recognize that. For me he's still the Kaiser.'

'So what are you going to do?'

'I'm going to write to the Kaiser asking him to absolve me.'

One Sunday he proudly showed me the reply from the Kaiser granting him the request. The letter was signed Wilhelm 11 IR

Instead of 'IR', I read, '*Im Ruhestand.*'

Everyone roared with laughter. IR is the usual German abbreviation for 'retired.'

'No, not "*Im Ruhestand*" but "*Imperator, Rex*", exclaimed Müller. 'The Kaiser, like me, does not recognize his forced abdication.' After this, Müller dressed in the uniform of a stormtrooper.

* * *

Before the First World War Müller lived in German East Africa (now Tanzania). At dinner he told us: 'This was the best time of my life. The English always criticized us for the way we treated the natives, but they were unfair. For example, one of my servants stole some rice, so I gave him a choice: either get a whipping or go without food for 24 hours. And what did this Negro choose? A whipping! The English press said we beat natives, but I gave him a choice and look what he chose.' As a child this argument impressed me.

* * *

In 1936 Vati remarried and moved to his wife's flat. During the pogrom of November 1938 he was put into Sachsenhausen concentration camp. Tante Trude, his wife, asked all their Gentile friends for assistance except the Müllers. 'I know they won't help. If they wanted to, they could contact us. They know we're in trouble,' she said.

* * *

In 1946, whilst I was in the army, the Search Department of the World Jewish Congress forwarded a letter to me addressed to my father who had died a few months earlier. It was from Herr Müller. It was many pages long. Here are some extracts:

> During the war I joined the *Reichskolonialbund* [a Nazi organization advocating the return of all former German colonies]. I travelled throughout Germany and gave lectures. It was very interesting. After Stalingrad, when Goebbels wanted us to concentrate on total war, this organization was disbanded and I worked in the occupied territories in the east. Now I'm back home but because I've been a party member my house has been taken from me. Not only are the leaders punished, but also people like me who were only nominal members and who only joined the party in order to earn a living. I've started de-Nazification proceedings but because of feelings of hate and revenge this is a difficult process. In the administration here in the Russian sector of Berlin there are so many victims from concentration camps that I may not succeed in getting my house back. I'm asking you to help me. I'd like you to swear

on oath that I helped you under the Nazis in order to demonstrate my anti-fascist convictions.

I was in a dilemma. I certainly did not want a Nazi to re-establish himself. On the other hand, he did help Vati when he was in need. I sent the following statement:

I herewith state that my deceased father Paul Prager had lived in the years 1929–1936 with the family Müller as a paying guest. I know Mr Müller helped my father financially. He gave him lodging and food for several years without receiving any recompense, even though he himself had been in financial difficulties. Mr Müller did this, although he knew my father was a Jew, for reasons of friendship. In my opinion Mr Müller joined the Nazi Party for idealistic and not criminal reasons.

Before my statement reached Herr Müller, the Russians had arrested him and put him into Sachsenhausen, the same camp where Vati had been in November 1938.

23   The Time of My Life

'I'm going to be rich.' I was sitting in the Cosmos café in Finchley Road chatting with friends of the Jewish Youth Group.

'How's that?'

'The Americans pay £8 per week plus food, accommodation and uniform. Here I'm getting £4 and have to look after myself and pay rent. I'll also get a ration of 200 cigarettes per week and I don't smoke.'

'How's that going to help?'

'I can sell them on the black market.'

'Nice way to start an army career.'

'Everybody does it.'

I joined the American army as a civilian in uniform the day Germany surrendered. After British wartime austerity it took me some time to get used to the abundance of food served in US army restaurants. Like many others from Britain I developed a rash which doctors attributed to a change in diet from starch to plenty of meat. It seemed to me I had entered the land of milk and honey. At the PX store I bought everything available – tins of food for my mother, and sheets, towels and even underwear to send home to England. After more than 50 years I still wear an old US army jacket and army boots for gardening. In Berlin I went to the opera and theatre twice a week, always in the best seats, while in London I could just about afford the gallery.

The US army considered the task of postal censorship very important. Apart from trying to locate war criminals and black marketeers (never mind that almost all American soldiers were engaged in this), our task was to gauge public opinion. What was the German reaction to the Nürnberg war criminal trials? How did German firms in the Russian Zone become Soviet institutions overnight with a Russian managing director? The British and American press were full of reports on occupied Germany, and in particular on Berlin. Private travel was not allowed. Germans were not permitted to send letters abroad. We were the only people to give firsthand information.

In Berlin I had lunch at the Allied Kommandatura and rubbed shoulders with Russian and American generals. I, a lonely refugee who had lived in a furnished room and counted for nothing in England, was quite suddenly thrown into the centre of activity of the world powers and I was part of that activity.

* * *

I had known Eva for several months. She was German and lived with her mother in a furnished room. I visited her once a week and was always warmly welcomed.

'Hello Peter. *Wie geht's?*'

'I've brought something different today.'

'It smells lovely. What is it?'

'The PX opened a bakery and we can buy fresh white bread every day.'

'We haven't had white bread for years.'

Since her mother was always present, my sexual advances were rather restricted. Eventually Eva found a quiet spot in a nearby park, and we were to embark on our sexual adventure, my first ever. I was very excited. My mates wished me luck. The evening arrived and as soon as Eva and her mother had devoured the food I had brought, I said, 'Let's go'. And off we went to the park.

When we had finished, instead of feeling elated, I was disgusted with myself. I never saw her again. My upbringing had been such that sex gave me a feeling of revulsion. Fortunately this wore off and soon I had relations with other girls.

My steadiest friend was Carla, a Czech Jewish girl from England who worked in the office with me. She was short and thick-set and not particularly pretty. But she was keen on me and invited me for coffee at her flat. I knocked and the door opened. She was in pyjamas. I looked rather disconcerted.

'Come in Peter,' she said, leading me straight into her bedroom, 'I don't beat about the bush.' Before I could collect myself she had seduced me. She had another boyfriend who was a captain in the Yugoslav army. He brought her caviar from the Russian PX. She didn't like it, so while I was in bed with her she gave me caviar rolls to munch.

Ilse was a Danish girl. I only spent one night with her. She was keen to get married to an American.

'Which state do you come from?' she asked me in bed.

'I don't come from any state. I come from London.'

'What, London England?'

'Yes, of course.' We never met again.

Really, I had fallen in love with another girl, Edith. She had black hair, brown eyes and a sophisticated look – to me she was irresistibly attractive. We worked in the same room and had our meals together. Her parents had also survived in Berlin, and we had much in common.

'There's a Beethoven concert on Saturday. Will, you come?' I asked her.

'Sorry, I'm otherwise engaged.' Every approach to go out with her was rebuffed.

Finally she confessed: 'I know what you want Peter. I like you, but I've already got a boyfriend. If it should break up I'll go with you. I'm sure you understand.' I was devastated. The other girls meant nothing to me. I had many sleepless nights over Edith.

24   *False Gods*

'Do you feel ill? You look as if you have a temperature. Here, have an aspirin.' A *Kapo* (foreman) said this to Vati in Sachsenhausen concentration camp in November 1938. The SS had made communists foremen over Jewish prisoners thinking they were bound to maltreat Jewish 'capitalists'. When Vati was released, the *Kapo* said: 'Remember me and my comrades when you are free.'

I was greatly inspired by Stalingrad. Though not a communist, I sympathized with them. I read the *Daily Worker*. In 1945 when I went to Germany as a postal censor I wanted to think well of the Red Army. Ilya Ehernbury had written: 'Communism has created a "New Soviet Man"'.

* * *

We received the first letters from the Soviet Zone:

'I must tell you, when the Russians came I could not escape the fate of everyone. All the women in our street were raped.'

'We blackened our faces and made ourselves look old. It didn't help.'

'The soldier asked me for my watch. I didn't have one. So I suffered the same as everyone else.'

Tante Else, who had hidden under the Nazis for two years, now in her sixties: 'They ransacked our house and took everything. They didn't care about Nazis or anti-Nazis. I had to hide for several weeks until the rape and plunder subsided.'

A Berlin official: 'Fifty per cent of all women in Berlin have been raped, and ten per cent of these have contracted VD. Penicillin is not issued to the German population.'

The newly constituted Berlin Senate passed a law: 'Because of the special circumstance pertaining in the city, doctors will not be prosecuted for performing abortions.'

I visited my parents in St Hedwig's Hospital. A nurse explains: 'All patients on the first floor women's ward are rape victims.'

A tailor, who lived at Nollendorf Platz: 'I was a youth leader in the socialist youth movement before the Nazis. When I became a POW in Russia, as a "good" German I was transferred to a special camp for anti-Nazis where conditions were superior. I returned to Germany wanting to foster friendship between us and the Soviets. At home I found that my wife and daughter had been raped. I just feel hatred for the Russians.'

* * *

Back in England, I had contact with Herr Kunze in the German Democratic Republic. He managed some property which I had inherited. One day he wrote: 'Could you find a pen friend for my son? He wants to learn English.'

Marion, the daughter of a local communist was eager to correspond with him. She wrote: 'Our newspapers write about oppression in your country. I don't believe it. What is the truth?' Despite repeated requests she did not get a reply to this question. Finally she wrote: 'In the name of youth, please tell me about conditions in your country.'

His reply contained two lines which were crossed out and made illegible. Marion, who was an Oxford undergraduate asked one of the Oxford laboratories to decipher the lines. They read: 'Regarding your question about conditions in my country, I cannot tell the truth.' She was shattered. Not because of what he had written but because he had crossed it out. He was afraid to say he was afraid to write the truth.

25   Dotheboyshall

'You're a "Master" now. Never use the word "Teacher". That word is good enough for the council school down the road. We are keeping up standards while the Labour government is ruining our country. Our class will have to get us out of the rut.' These were the introductory remarks made in 1947 by Mr Holt, the headmaster of my first teaching post at Eastcote School, Redhill, Surrey, a private boarding school. I had been accepted for teacher training under the post-war Emergency Training Scheme. There was a waiting list of more than a year and I had looked for a post as an unqualified teacher. At Eastcote I was soon appointed housemaster.

Mr Holt had just been demobbed from the Indian army where he had been a major in the Education Corps in charge of libraries. He had an Oxford degree, was not qualified as a teacher and had bought the school as an investment. He looked down on teachers who were state trained. I had to listen to his harangue every day, even at mealtimes.

'But surely there's some merit in the welfare state,' I interjected.

'You've been taken in by socialist propaganda. We've won the war but the Labour government is dragging us down to the Russian level.' He spent a lot of time telling me how horrible the Russians were, but not a word about the Nazis. He behaved as if Britain and Germany had been allies fighting the Russians.

Eastcote School was the cheapest private school in Surrey. We had 100 boarders and as many day-boys. Parents were convinced their children were receiving a better education than in state schools because they had to pay. Pretentious parents sent their children there. Others boarded their children to get them out of the way, like seven-year-old Ian MacGregor whose parents sent him to Surrey all the way from

Glasgow. The boy's behaviour was atrocious and he became almost unmanageable. He constantly picked quarrels with other children, often ending in fist fights. However the matron succeeded in taming him, and her cure was so simple. When he was particularly obnoxious she said: 'Ian come here!' Then she cuddled him saying 'Good boy,' and he immediately calmed down. Soon he sat patiently outside her room and waited until she had time for him to sit on her lap to be cuddled.

During winter one day we had a heavy snowfall, and on afternoon duty I decided to organize the boys into snow-sweeping gangs. I distributed snow-clearing equipment. After a few minutes there was shouting: 'Sir! Come quickly!' Ian had been using a pitchfork and one tine had gone through his big toe and was protruding out the other side. I was terrified. I withdrew the tine, carried the boy to the kitchen and put his foot into disinfectant. The doctor bandaged him up and the foot healed completely. I was afraid the parents would allege negligence, but they were not worried and they did not even visit him while he was convalescing.

As the school was cheap, the headmaster could not engage experienced staff. He even skimped on food for boys and staff. I later discovered he went to the larder every night before going to bed to have a good feed. Every potential pupil was surveyed for size. Mr Holt would tell us: 'Today I interviewed an enormous boy. He would eat us out of house and home. I told the parents we were full up.' We were a school of small children. This worked all right until the arrival of Cross. The previous owner of the school had warned Mr Holt about this boy. Though suitably small when he joined, he grew and grew. Now he was 15 and a giant – and he ate like one. Every day when the children filed into the dining room Mr Holt would stand at the door, eyeing Cross furiously. He seemed to size him up as though he could detect a daily growth. Cross was a very happy boy and always asked cheerfully: 'Can I have some more, please?' This had to be given grudgingly but to Mr Holt's extreme annoyance, it encouraged other children to do the same.

I was given a garret to sleep in. I moved in on Sunday in order to start on Monday. My room led straight to the loft and as I unpacked my cases I wanted to put the empty ones in the loft. Unlike England, in Germany all loft floors are boarded so that one can walk around. As I stepped into the loft I walked on the plaster, expecting it to take my weight. Suddenly it began to give way. Before I realized what was happening my feet had broken through the plaster. They were dangling into the room below while I was held straddled over a beam. Apart from the shock of breaking through the ceiling, I was even more terrified when I noticed that my feet were dangling right above the headmaster's head. He was sitting on the settee with his wife, watching television. They both jumped up, wiping the plaster off their clothes.

'I'm sorry,' I began, 'I don't know how this happened. I was just walking in the loft trying to put my cases away when the floor gave way.'

'Prager, there is no floor in the loft,' he shouted back. 'I've just decorated this ceiling! I only finished today.'

This conversation took place while I was still dangling from the ceiling. I pulled myself up and ran downstairs to apologize. I was completely distraught and very much afraid he would give me the sack straight away. However, with school starting the following day Mr Holt needed me as much as I needed the job, and I started on Monday as scheduled.

The Science Lesson

One of the subjects I had to teach was science, though my knowledge of it was nil. My last science lesson had been when I was 15 and I had never undertaken any experiments myself. The headmaster gave me a book, *Scientific Experiments for Children*, and said to me: 'Just get on with it'.

I did remember one experiment which we had done at school. The teacher had demonstrated how coal gas was formed. I decided to do the same. While I demonstrated, I explained to the class: 'I put a small piece of coal into this test tube. I fix a Bunsen burner underneath. I leave a small opening at the top of the tube for the gas to escape. I light the escaping gas with a match.' While I was doing this I didn't notice that the opening in the cork was blocked.

'Boys, can you see the gas escaping?'

'Yes!' they shouted.

I put a match to the opening still not realizing that it was blocked. I could see more and more gas accumulating but I could not produce a flame from the opening. Suddenly there was a huge bang. The cork flew to the back of the classroom and the test tube broke into a thousand pieces scattering splinters everywhere.

There was a tremendous excitement among the boys. 'Sir made a real explosion.' They never realized that the experiment had gone wrong. I immediately became a hero. 'Good old Sir,' they said. Soon news spread among the other boys and the staff, and Mr Holt congratulated me on making my science lessons so interesting. But after that I stopped performing scientific experiments.

* * *

I was obliged to teach Religious Knowledge. Though the head knew I was Jewish, he did not seem to care. He gave me a Bible and, as with Science, said, 'Get on with it'. My knowledge of the New Testament was non-existent, so I concentrated on the Old Testament and managed to teach one lesson per week for a whole year.

* * *

Another member of staff had been a sergeant-major and like Mr Holt had just been demobbed. He was a housemaster and taught Hygiene. He was not teacher-trained either and was the school's handyman. When he gave a lesson the rest of the building resounded with his tremendous voice: 'Flies are the carriers of disease. Never let them settle on food.' I heard this sentence every day and wondered when he might turn to another topic, but this was never to happen.

One morning most of the boarders appeared at the breakfast table with spots on their faces. The doctor could not diagnose anything serious. Mr Holt thought he knew the cause. The matron (the sergeant-major's wife) bathed the boys two at a time in the same bath water. Mr Holt maintained that this was dirty, and the cause of the boys' spots. He ordered:

'Give them a cold shower every morning!' But the matron refused:

'That is unhealthy,' she maintained. 'The boys have spots because they are deprived of fresh fruit.'

Mr Holt was furious and gave the couple notice. I became the new housemaster, and the parting-shot of the sergeant-major to me was: 'Prager, if you give them cold showers they'll catch pneumonia.' I was in a terrible dilemma. Should I or should I not carry out the headmaster's orders? If I carried them out and the boys fell ill, would I be held responsible? Could I give as an excuse that I acted under orders? The Nürnberg war criminal trials had just finished and had established that a wrong action can never be excused because one acted under orders. What was I to do? I asked Onkel Jean, the doctor. His advice was: 'A cold shower normally does not do any harm, but it is not a good idea to start this in winter.' But it was January! Fortunately the problem solved itself. The spots disappeared of their own accord and Mr Holt forgot all about cold showers.

Football

Every Wednesday afternoon the school closed for football. The staff had a free afternoon, except me. I had to take the entire school to Redhill Common and organize a football game. I had no knowledge of the game; I had never played football and knew nothing of the rules.

The headmaster explained: 'It's quite simple. Let the two captains pick their teams. When they're ready on the field they'll look at you and you just blow the whistle. During the game the boys might shout "foul", then immediately blow the whistle. Wait a minute or two and the boys will shout, "ready, sir", then blow the whistle again. If the game goes on for more than five minutes without anybody shouting "foul", blow the whistle anyway. The boys will know what to do.'

I did as instructed and to my surprise everything worked out the way Mr Holt had predicted. No boy ever found out that I knew nothing of the rules. Nevertheless after a few weeks the headmaster decided to take over from me. Parents of day-boys complained that their sons simply went home, instead of watching the game. I couldn't supervise 100 spectators as well.

* * *

There was a maximum of 15 pupils per class and I had little difficulty in keeping discipline. When a boy behaved badly I made him stand in a corner with his hands folded over his head. One day I did this with Robinson. After about 15 minutes he leaned his head against the wall. I thought he was having a rest and told him to stand straight. There was no response. I repeated my order but still there was no response. I shouted: 'Robinson, if you don't stand straight I'll send you to the headmaster to be caned.' He didn't move.

The rest of the class began to take an interest in the affair, staring at me and Robinson, wondering who would win. My authority was at stake and I grabbed Robinson by the hair in order to pull him off the wall. His face was white and his eyes closed. He had fainted. The force of my pull had made his body lose balance and he fell backwards. I caught him in my arms and carried him to the nearest desk. He came to immediately.

'Are you alright?' I was very anxious. He remembered what he had to do and at once got up and ran to the corner saying, 'Sorry sir'. I pulled him back, very gently this time, and asked him to sit down. He didn't understand. 'It's alright, Robinson. You've been sufficiently punished. Just go back to your place.' This episode gave me the reputation of being a stern disciplinarian.

Mrs Holt

The headmaster's wife was a young and pretty woman who took an immediate dislike to me. I think she hated Germans as well as Jews, so I was irredeemably lost. She decided to fight me with petty chicaneries. We used the same bathroom and whenever I was sitting in the bath she would knock and ask, 'Please, could you hand me my toothbrush?' This happened with such regularity that one day I decided to put her toothbrush on the floor outside the bathroom before I went inside. On that occasion I heard grunts of anger outside and when I came out I heard her screaming in her bedroom about 'these impertinent German manners'.

In my garret there was no heating, and in winter it became bitterly cold. I asked for permission to use my electric heater. Mr Holt said he would have to ask his business partner first. The next day I was told that I couldn't use my electric heater because they had not allowed for this extra expense. Mr Holt told me I could use his office for dressing and undressing. I accepted this offer but his wife did not approve. Every time I wanted to dress or undress she was in the office cleaning and would not move. In the end I gave up. I had defeated her with the toothbrush and she had won the battle over dressing in the office. I went back to my cold garret.

The Head Boy at the time was an extremely pretty 16-year-old called George. His long fair hair and blue eyes made him look like a girl, and his face looked like Donatello's David. His pleasant, amiable manner made him popular with staff and pupils alike. He was a model scholar, always attentive and well behaved, one of the few preparing for the School Certificate. Mrs Holt said: 'I'll see to it that he won't fail.' How did she do this?

Mr Holt had two vices: beer and betting. Every Thursday afternoon he went to Lingfield Races whilst the evenings he spent in the nearby pub. After closing time he entered the house, staggered to the cellar and continued to drink. At first his wife strongly objected to his behaviour but eventually they came to an understanding: he could do what he liked, provided she could do what she liked. What did she like? I returned to the school for a visit after I had left, and then I found out.

It was a Thursday and Mr Holt was in Lingfield. Mrs Holt was just returning from swimming with George. Nothing suspicious about that really. As George had only recently been in the water his lips were bluish-red and he looked even more like a girl.

'George you look as if you wear lipstick'. My remark was followed by an embarrassed silence.

Matron gave me a nudge, I heard sniggers from some boys and Mrs Holt remarked: 'Prager, you always manage to say just the wrong thing.' Whereupon she and George disappeared upstairs.

I turned to matron: 'What's going on?'

'Obviously you don't know,' she said. We went to her room where she enlightened me: 'She has seduced George. They're always seen together, he sits next to her at mealtimes and they go out together.'

'And what does her husband say?' I asked.

'Nothing. He knows but he doesn't care. As soon as he goes to Lingfield or the pub, they go to her bedroom and lock the door. She says she gives him private lessons and does not want to be disturbed.'

'And what about the boys?' I enquired. 'Oh, they think it's funny and make jokes about it. The staff, of course, think it's disgusting, but what can you do?'

Mrs Holt's private lessons were very successful because George was the only boy who achieved the School Certificate that year.

* * *

During the last week of term a cricket match was arranged between the pupils and staff. The staff was so small that I was obliged to participate. I knew nothing of the game and was scared stiff in case I made a fool of myself in front of the entire school. Mr Holt again reassured me: 'You field at a spot where no ball is likely to reach. I promise you I'll declare before it's your turn to bat.' He kept his word and I never touched the ball during the game. It was the only game of cricket I played in my whole life.

On the day I left the school the headmaster shook hands with me and said: 'Prager, you've had a rough introduction to teaching. I can guarantee you can never have a worse job. Good luck for the future.' As a farewell present, I bought him a Left Book Club edition of a doctor's account of Auschwitz. I wanted him to clarify his ideas about the war.

Forty years later I went again to the spot in Station Road, Redhill, where the school had been situated. The school was no more; a new building had been erected called the Red Arrow Health Care Centre.

26   *Qualified Teaching*

Whilst in the US army I thought: 'What am I going to do when I leave? Go back to the rag trade? No, never! I want to study. But how? I've no money.' I saw an advert in the papers:

> Britain is desperately short of teachers. It has therefore been decided to introduce an emergency training scheme. For the first time students will get free tuition and a living allowance.

This was for me. I applied immediately and went for an interview whilst on leave in London.

I entered the interview room. The panel looked at me and I overheard the remark: 'First time we've seen someone like him.'

I wondered what they meant – that I was Jewish, German, or dressed in American Army uniform?

'Why do you want to become a teacher?'

I said, brilliantly I thought, 'I like travelling and would do more of it in the long holidays. And with the short hours I could go to concerts and theatres.' The members of the interviewing board looked at each other and there was a pause.

'Don't you like children?'

I answered quickly and with emphasis: 'Of course I've always liked children. I like playing with my nephew and niece.'

'Thank you. We'll let you know of our decision.'

I was accepted at Didsbury Training College in 18 months' time. There was a colossal shortage of teachers in 1947.

Teaching Practice

My first teaching practice was in Ashton-under-Lyne, a mining village in the Pennines. It was a tough area where schools had discipline problems.

'Where do you come from?' was the first question of the staff when they noticed my foreign accent.

'From Germany. I am a Jewish refugee.' The staff looked at each other.

The PE teacher was the only person who smiled and talked to me: 'You know, the staff don't like you.'

'So I noticed.'

'They don't think a foreigner should teach our children.'

'I thought it was something like that.'

'They've given you the most difficult classes.'

'I've realized that too.'

'They want you to fail.'

At lunchtime the deputy head said to me: 'I'm sorry we haven't room for you to eat with us. I'll prepare a table for you in one of the classrooms.' During the two weeks I was there I had to take my meals in a classroom all by myself.

At the end of my teaching practice I was called to the headmaster: 'Nowadays many unsuitable people want to enter the teaching profession. Schools would be better served if these people realized that teaching was not for them.'

Throughout my life I have suffered from an inability to take hints. I agreed with everything the headmaster said.

Back from teaching practice I was called to the principal, Mr Body, OBE.

'Teaching is not your strength, is it?' he said.

'I like it very much.'

'We've had a bad report from the school. You'll have to work harder if you want to remain on the course.'

Fortunately I was luckier with my next teaching practice and succeeded in passing.

* * *

Mr Body was very much concerned about morality in our mixed college. In the evenings he stood behind bushes outside the students' entrance, watching which male student associated with which female student. He could not have approved of my associates, nor of my general conduct, judging by what he wrote in my college testimonial, which I have treasured to this day.

He is a student who has certainly benefited from living in a residential community throughout the year, and I hope that his attitude towards his work, both in the classroom and in the staffroom, will reflect that clear appreciation of social values which he must certainly have encountered amongst his fellow students during the last year.

St Chad's Secondary Modern School

'Welcome Mr Prager! We've been waiting for years to fill this post. People don't like teaching the children of dockers in a slummy district like Tilbury. It's too tough for them. We're glad you've come to us.' These were the only pleasant remarks I was to hear for some time; they were made by Miss Hall, Headmistress of St Chad's Secondary Modern School, Tilbury, Essex. Due to my college testimonial I could only be allocated to a school where nobody else wanted to teach.

There was icy silence when I entered the staff room. 'So you're German,' said Mr Jones the deputy head.

'I'm a Jewish refugee,' I replied. It was important to add this so soon after the war.

'I must introduce you to Mr Williams,' he said with a twinkle in his eye. 'He's just been demobbed from the Palestine Police Force.'

Williams looked at me cold-eyed. 'These Palestinian Jews are terrible. You can't trust them. They talk to you in the friendliest possible way, and when you aren't looking they shoot you in the back.'

'I suppose they've ruined Palestine,' said Jones.

'Actually they haven't. They just hated us British. I couldn't get home quick enough. Long live Mosley!'

'And this is Mr Bradley, our PE teacher. He lives in Southend.'

'Hello Prager. Southend is a lovely place. Unfortunately it is beginning to look like Tel Aviv.'

'You wouldn't talk like that if you'd been with the army out in India as I have,' said Jones. 'If you've lived with the wogs, you'd agree that they are worse than Jews.'

* * *

Teaching at St Chad's did provide some light entertainment. The girls I taught chatted a lot, but there was no disorder. On one occasion they seemed to be in a particularly excited state, passing notes to each other and giggling. I didn't know what was going on and tried to catch the notes. They were very keen to prevent me from getting hold of one. 'No, sir!' they screamed when at last I snatched one. The girls held their breath, looking at me and at each other. What did the note say? It read: 'His fly is undone.' They were right. I crawled behind my desk and zipped myself up. I wanted to disappear but I got up and carried on teaching as if nothing had happened. In future before I entered the classroom I always made sure that this disaster never happened again.

On another occasion the girls became excited again and I saw them passing notes. Discreetly I looked down at my trousers – no mishap there. What was the matter? I finally succeeded in catching a note: 'He's had a haircut.' I decided to have my hair cut at frequent intervals after that so that it would not cause any more commotion.

What could I do to get out of this school? The only thing for it was to get better qualifications. I decided to work for a degree. Grants for full time study were almost impossible to obtain in those days, so I took a correspondence course for an economics degree and succeeded several years later.

Bushy Bit

'What are you doing here?' His loud resonant voice penetrated the entire building. The parent whom he was addressing looked rather frightened.

'I'm looking for the headmaster,' she replied hesitantly.

'I am the headmaster. Have you an appointment?'

'No, but I should like to make one.'

'You've no business to enter this building without prior appointment. Leave at once.'

'Can't I make an appointment now?'

'Only by letter or phone. Will you leave immediately.'

The parent, having been sufficiently cowed, left without further ado.

Mr Reid-Jones, the headmaster of Aveley Secondary

Modern School, was a large bespectacled man who strode around his school as though surveying a huge workplace of slaves. British schools were known for their authoritarian structure at this time – it was 1956. The head teacher was supreme, and criticism by anyone – staff, pupils or parents – was discouraged.

When Mr Reid-Jones became head of Aveley Secondary School his absolute power went to his head. A resolute commander-in-chief must plan his battle positions in solitude. He told his secretary to move her desk from his office to the deputy head's room. The deputy head was told to use the staff room for his work. The deputy's duties were few because the head made all important decisions himself. He constructed a master timetable which never changed during his tenure. Every year new staff had to fit into the timetable, not vice versa, even if this meant they had to teach subjects of which they had insufficient knowledge. Staff meetings consisted of announcements only. 'As from next Monday school will start five minutes earlier and morning break will be extended by five minutes.' 'As from today two staff instead of one will patrol the corridors at lunch time.'

He succeeded in creating such an atmosphere of fear that none dared contradict him. But one young woman had the courage to say: 'I don't agree with this decision.' She paid dearly for it, however, because when she applied for another post and the prospective employer asked for a reference, Mr Reid-Jones wrote just one sentence: 'Miss Brown has been working in my school for three years.' Eventually half the staff had the courage to sign a letter of complaint to the education office. The letter was acknowledged but no action was taken. In those days, unless a head teacher assaulted a pupil, his position was safe in our English education system.

The school was situated on a wooded hillock, and the postal address was Bushy Bit. Many children called the school just 'Bushy Bit'. Mr Reid-Jones strongly objected to this name – it had certain connotations he didn't like. As soon as he heard a child say 'Bushy Bit' he called him over.

'What is the name of this school?'

'Bushy Bit.'

'No,' he would roar. 'Try again.'

'Bushy Bit, sir.' The child was near to tears.

'Come to my office,' he commanded the sobbing child. If the pupil still could not think of the proper name he would get 100 lines: 'I must remember this school is called Aveley Secondary School.'

* * *

Having just obtained my degree I applied for a post at the school. I knew nothing of Reid-Jones diktats. He phoned me the day he received my application asking me to come for an interview the next day. I was pleasantly surprised at his eagerness and took no heed of a colleague's warning that 'he needed to be eager if he wanted people to teach at his school.' I accepted the offer of a job. I did not realize what was in store for me.

On my first day I was presented with a timetable in which one third of lessons were Religious Instruction though I was employed as Geography teacher. I went to Mr Reid-Jones' office.

'I wonder whether you made a mistake when you gave me RI.'

'How's that?'

'You see, I'm Jewish.'

He looked at me. It took some time to register. Then he let forth a roar of laughter.

'Excuse me,' I said taken aback by this outburst, 'I assume you don't now wish me to teach this subject.'

'Prager, as a teacher you have to be prepared to teach any subject on the curriculum. I certainly expect you to teach the timetable as I have given it to you.'

Mr Reid-Jones considered the fact that a Jew was teaching RI in his school the best joke for years. 'A Jew teaching religion in my school,' he kept on saying. He couldn't get over it. For weeks whenever he met me in the corridor, he had a little laugh and I could hear under his breath the words, 'Jew, RI.' This was the second time I had been obliged to teach religion. I was entitled to refuse but I didn't want to create a fuss and, as before, I taught the Old Testament. Nobody cared.

* * *

Mr Reid-Jones had written several travel books while he was supposed to be managing his school. He locked himself into his office and then wrote away for hours with no-one daring to interrupt him.

He also fancied himself an art expert. He went to auctions hoping to discover a masterpiece. At breaktime he would often call me to his office. One day he said, 'Prager, come to my office. I picked this up at a house in Billericay. What do you think?' He then showed me a picture which was so dirty that one could hardly recognize anything. 'It just needs cleaning. It looks early nineteenth century, doesn't it?' Why did he pick on me? Perhaps he had an idea that Jews must know all about art. I knew nothing and tried to hide my ignorance. 'Yes, you're right. It probably is early- or mid-nineteenth century.' Such remarks satisfied him. When caught in this way, as the bell rang for the new lesson, I would turn towards the door to go back to my class – he was very keen for teachers to start their class punctually, however, art took precedence. He would tell me to sit down, that the deputy head would see to my class – she had instructions to supervise classes when the teacher was detained by him. Then he would spend an entire lesson discussing art with me.

Years afterwards I saw him being interviewed on television. He had discovered a Turner valued at £250,000.

Reid-Jones was a great patriot. Each school assembly started with a hymn and finished with 'God Save the Queen', 'Land of my Fathers' (he was Welsh) or the 'British Grenadiers'. In the 1950s this latter song was still in the school hymnbook, and the children sang the bloodthirsty lines with relish:

> When'ever we are commanded
> To storm the palisades,
> Our leaders march with fuses,
> And we with hand grenades;
> We throw them from the glacis
> About the enemies' ears,
> Sing tow row row row row row The British Grenadiers

Within just a few months of arriving at the school I started looking for another job and, much to my relief, soon left.

27   *Changing Course*

'From your application form I can see that you've just obtained a degree in economic history.' The headmaster of Aveley Technical High School was a softly spoken, elderly man of medium height whose sympathetic eyes immediately put me at ease.

'Yes, I have.'

'I suppose that's what you want to teach.'

'Yes, I do.'

'From your application form I see that you were born in Germany.'

'Yes, in Berlin.'

'What's your German like?'

'I'm bilingual.'

'Good. Actually I don't need an economic history teacher. As a technical school our emphasis is on languages. Have you ever thought of teaching German?'

'No, I haven't.'

'Well, that's what I want you to do. We can offer you a post to teach German. Go home and think about it. I'll give you a week. Let us know whether you'll accept the post.'

Aveley Technical High School was a newly built selective school. You had to pass the 11+ exam to get in. The *Times Educational Supplement* had carried the following advert: 'Staff required for this new school. State subject offered.' After eight years at secondary modern schools I felt I needed a break.

However, teaching German had never occurred to me and I had no paper qualifications. I was not prepared for this offer so I had to do some quick thinking. A new school opens up new career prospects and I really wanted to teach there.

In order to teach a language, empathy for the country and it's people is essential. But I hated Germany. When I applied for naturalization I had written in the application form for present nationality: stateless. The Home Office wrote back: 'According to our records you are German. Why have you filled in stateless?' I replied, 'As a Jew I cannot be German.' I even refused to teach my children German. What was I to do?

I went to the Goethe Institute and started to read extensively. There was the 20 July plot in which thousands of Germans were killed trying to overthrow Hitler; the White Rose which spread anti-Nazi propaganda among Münich students; and I read about the thousands of Germans who were martyred as Christians. I realised that for every Jew who lived underground there were ten to twenty Germans who had helped them and risked a concentration camp. Onkel Richard and Tante Else had given me a detailed account of their experience living in hiding. According to the Berlin Museum 'Resistance to National Socialism', as many as 5,000 Jews lived illegally in Berlin. That meant that perhaps 50,000 Berliners had risked their lives to rescue them.

The book *Der lautlose Aufstand* by Günter Weisenborn mentions that 225,000 Germans had been sentenced by the courts for political offences during the period 1933–1939. In addition, one million Germans had been in concentration camps for long or short periods. This does not include Jews. A secret Gestapo document reported that on 10 April 1939 the following were in custody for political reasons: 162,734 in protective custody, 27,369 waiting to be tried for political reasons, 112,432 in prisons tried for political offences. Another Gestapo report said that in April, May and June 1944 a total of 20,748 Germans were arrested for political reasons. This happened before the 20 July attempt on Hitler's life when the number arrested rose steeply.

And then there was Onkel Franz. Onkel Franz was German. As he was part of my family it never occurred to me that as a Gentile he was a member of the master race.

I wrote to the headmaster: 'I hereby accept the post of German teacher at your school.' I have taught German all my life.

John Martin

The success or otherwise of my German teaching I was able to gauge many years later after I had left the school. My wife Sylvia and I spent a weekend in Amsterdam. We were sitting in a café when Sylvia said to me: 'There's a man over there shaking his head and gazing at you. Either there's something wrong with him or he wants to attract your attention.'

I looked around. 'His face is familiar but I can't place him.'

The man got up and came towards me. 'Are you Peter Prager?'

'Yes. Who are you?'

'I'm John Martin, don't you remember me?'

'You must be a former pupil of mine.'

'Yes, Aveley Technical High School.'

'So you learnt German with me.'

'Indeed, I did.'

'How many years ago?'

'I left school in 1978.'

We shook hands and embraced, oblivious of our surroundings. The conversation was carried on in a loud voice and the customers in the café stopped talking and listened to us. They were smiling and they seemed pleased at our reunion. John introduced me to his wife and children and we sat together and exchanged reminiscences. John had passed an interpreters' exam in Bonn and was now an employee of the German government.

I needed no higher praise.

28   Liberal Studies

'Did you write this letter?' The principal of East Ham College of Technology held the letter column of the *Guardian* newspaper in front of me.

'Yes, I wrote that letter.'

'You have maligned the college.'

'No, I haven't.'

'Yes, you have.'

'How?'

'You have accused the North Thames Gas Board of racial discrimination in their employment policy. They send their students to us, so we are involved. I don't know why you as a Jew should be concerned with racism. The Old Testament is full of it. Will you promise never again to write such a letter?'

Ignoring the insult for the time being, I said: 'I cannot possibly give such a promise. It is my democratic right to write to the press whenever I feel like it.'

The principal was getting excited and turning red with anger. 'Mr Prager. I have to tell you I am sorry now that I promoted you from Lecturer Grade 1 to Lecturer Grade 2. You will hear more from me. You can go.'

I had been working at the college for three years. I was co-ordinator of Liberal Studies. Many of our students were gas fitters and the staff was appalled by their racism. It was the time of Enoch Powell's speech of 'rivers of blood' and the march by dockers and meat porters from the East End to Parliament in support of him. We tried in vain to combat this prejudice. I gave a course on the rise of Nazism. 'There's no similarity between the Jews and the wogs,' my students told me. 'You don't live among them.' The gas fitting apprentices were recruited from Hackney and Brixton and yet not a single coloured student was among them. The government had just passed new legislation outlawing racial discrimination in employment. I had written to the *Guardian* stating there was a prima facie case of discrimination by the North Thames Gas Board.

* * *

Liberal Studies was a new subject. It was conceived by Her Majesty's Inspectorate for Further Education, and was meant to give students in technical colleges a liberal outlook on life. It was thought if ten years of secondary modern schooling had not broadened their outlook, one lesson per week at college would do it. There was no prescribed syllabus; it was left to each college and to each teacher to work one out. Any contemporary or cultural issue could be introduced. Our staff consisted of an enthusiastic young team of lecturers, most of whom had no teaching qualifications. This was not considered necessary in those days, so a lot of people were attracted to teaching who had bees in their bonnet which they wanted to let loose on their students.

They were engaged on a freelance basis. Audrey was a nurse and she was employed to teach First Aid. She was a left-wing socialist who spent her spare time going to demonstrations. It was 1968, the year of student sit-ins, Vietnam and CND protests. She belonged to the Committee of 100, the anti-nuclear lobby which believed in breaking the law to achieve their aim. I used to give her a lift to and from college. One day on the way home she said: 'I've asked John Taylor to speak to the students.'

'But he is an anarchist and a squatters' leader,' I replied with some apprehension.

'Yes, he was London's first squatter. He is squatting in Ilford and I know him very well.'

'What is he supposed to be talking about?'

'About squatting.'

'What has that got to do with First Aid?'

'He makes homeless people live more hygienically – that's First Aid.'

'Why didn't you ask for permission before inviting an outside speaker?'

'I don't need permission.'

When I got home and thought about it, I realized that, as I was the co-ordinator of Liberal Studies, I might be blamed for promoting anarchy. I became rather frightened and phoned Audrey. 'You must cancel the visit.'

'I'm not going to. I'm in charge of the class. In any case, John lives in a squat which has no telephone, so I can't reach him before he arrives in the morning.'

I went hot and cold when she said this, realizing that the meeting could not be cancelled. I said to her: 'Please do me just one favour. Don't tell anyone that you told me beforehand about the visit.'

'Yes, Peter, I'll promise you that.'

Next morning when I arrived at the college John Taylor was already there with his jeep to which were fixed huge posters saying 'Ilford Squat'. To my horror I discovered that Audrey had informed all the Liberal Studies lecturers to send their students to the hall 'for an important talk'. They all complied only too readily, pleased to get rid of their students for a lesson. I made myself scarce by pretending to do some work in another building. I emerged at breaktime and was immediately called to the Head of Department. 'Did you know that Audrey asked the anarchist John Taylor to the college?'

'You don't say,' I replied. 'When is he coming?'

'He's been. I've reported the matter to the principal. There will be repercussions.'

Audrey was called to the principal and lost her job.

* * *

Lecturers were often at a loss about what to teach. Pete solved the problem the easy way. His lesson was from 12 to 1 o'clock and he took his students to the pub until he was discovered and told not to come again. Shirley told her students to do their homework during their Liberal Studies lesson while she went to the canteen to have her lunch. She did this for six months until she was found out.

However John was no shirker; he intended to teach his students proper lessons. He had just obtained a sociology degree specializing in Social Awareness.

I said to him: 'I leave the topic you wish to teach entirely to you. The important thing is to interest the students.' Because the gas fitters presented discipline problems I gave him a class of girls learning secretarial skills. 'Remember, they've had a very narrow upbringing,' I said, and then left him to get on with it. I did not witness myself what I am relating now. I obtained the information from interviewing the girls after the event.

It was a hot summer's day. John arrived in shorts. A teacher in shorts? Well, it was the time of the Flower People and there was a tendency that 'everything goes'. It was John's second lesson with the girls.

Perched on a desk, John began: 'I want to talk about awareness.'

'Why do we wear clothes?' Silence. 'Well, why do we?'

'To protect us from the cold,' one girl said timidly.

'What, in this heat?' He took off his shirt. The girls stared at him, some giggling. 'We're all hypocrites. Most people say we wear clothes to protect us from the weather. But it's not true. It's sexual shame that makes us wear clothes. But why should we be ashamed of our bodies? Animals don't wear clothes, only humans do. It's all wrong. The Ancient Greeks weren't ashamed to show their bodies to each other.' While he was talking he unbuttoned his shorts and took them off. Then he took off his pants. The girl's eyes were starting out of their heads. 'I'm not worried standing like this in front of you. I want you to get rid of this feeling of awkwardness. I want you to become aware of yourself and of your neighbours. When you have your tea break I want you to discuss your feelings with each other.'

The next morning the college was inundated with protests from irate parents. Some girls handed in letters of complaints. The Head of Department asked me to investigate. John was immediately dismissed though he complained he had done nothing wrong. Other staff complained about him and the Liberal Studies section never recovered from this lesson.

The Ministry of Education had many complaints from employers who objected to sending their students to college for further technical training and then had Liberal Studies thrust upon them. A Ministry order was issued absolving colleges from the duty of teaching this subject in industrial training.

Diploma in Sociology

Our department was also responsible for the Diploma in Sociology. It was thought to be akin to Liberal Studies and I was put in charge. One of the lecturers was Carol, a young woman with a three-month-old baby girl. One day she arrived with the baby in a carrycot.

'I couldn't find a baby sitter. Do you mind if I bring her along?' Of course I didn't object.

She went into her classroom barefooted as was the custom for sociology lecturers in the 1960s. Her subject was Deviant Behaviour. As usual she sat in the middle and her students sat in a semi-circle around her. Suddenly the baby started to cry. Immediately Carol unbuttoned her blouse and breastfed the baby while continuing with the lecture. Satisfied after her feed, the baby then relieved herself. Carol held the baby away from her so she didn't get wet. A puddle formed on the floor and flowed towards the students. Everybody was fascinated. Where would it flow? Who would it touch? Can we shift chairs to avoid getting wet? Wouldn't it make too much noise? Carol, meanwhile, carried on as though nothing had happened. Fortunately the urine flow stopped before it reached any student.

When the lesson had finished nobody had listened to Carol's lecture and therefore had learnt nothing about deviant behaviour.

A student complained to me about the class. I said: 'If all of you write a letter of complaint, I can do something. Otherwise Carol will insist that students did not object.'

The next day the student told me: 'I can't get anyone to sign. The course depends on internal assessment and the students are afraid they will be penalized.'

29 Blackboard Jungle

The union representative of my new school greeted me: 'Welcome to Leyton, Peter. Are you NUT?'

'I've been a member for 30 years.'

'Good. I hope you'll join us on our action day.'

'What's that?' I asked apprehensively.

'The London branch has declared a one-day strike.'

'But it's unofficial. The executive has forbidden it.'

'If you wait for the union bosses to do something, you can wait until doomsday. We want action now. Salary increases are long overdue.'

'If the school is closed, mothers will have to stay at home to look after their kids. How can you, as a woman, sponsor this kind of action?'

'Peter, we all have to make sacrifices. The mothers will understand.'

'What about indiscipline? There's enough trouble already. The closure will upset the kids and we'll have a worse time.'

'Nonsense. Lack of discipline is society's fault. Until the system is changed the kids are bound to take it out on teachers. Whether we like it or not, the kids see us as the representatives of capitalism. But if we go on strike we show them that we can't be messed about.'

'I'm sorry, I couldn't disagree more. I'm not going on an unofficial strike.'

'That's a pity. You should show solidarity.'

* * *

Not a good start at my new school. In 1974 I became Head of the Languages Department of Leyton Senior High Boys' School. It was an inner-city social priority area school. A large percentage of the boys had been in trouble with the police and truancy was rife. I knew that my task of teaching German would not be easy. What had I let myself in for?

I was a great believer in comprehensive education; I had been chairman of Redbridge Comprehensive Schools Committee and helped in the abolition of the 11+ in the borough. I was keen to further comprehensives. Formerly the neighbourhood had been middle class, part of the stockbroker belt adjoining Epping Forest, but after the war tower blocks were built for people from the East End. As they moved in, the middle class people moved out, and the big houses became multi-family occupied. The school reflected the people who lived there. Its ex-pupils had done well in the professions – actor Derek Jacobi was an old boy. When I started teaching there some of the staff could remember him acting in school plays. Social deterioration started while the school was still a grammar school, and proceeded rapidly as it turned into a comprehensive.

Violence was rife, and occasionally it erupted against a teacher. As I walked past a classroom one day, a pupil and teacher were engaged in a fight. I rushed in to help. Almost daily fights occurred between pupils, and they were fights to the finish. If a teacher tried to separate them they both turned on the teacher, so when they had to be parted, a teacher had to call a colleague to help.

As a German teacher I was particularly vulnerable. On one occasion as I entered the building two boys raised their right arms and shouted: '*Heil Hitler!*' I complained to the Head and was told: 'These boys aren't quite normal. Don't take any notice of them. You take things too seriously.'

Everybody had to be politically correct. One day I reported that 'I had just seen a boy smashing a window. He ran off and I didn't know his name.' However, in my description of him I was not allowed to say he was black. This made detection more difficult.

Discipline deteriorated rapidly. During breaktime we didn't walk to the staff room along the corridor for fear of being jostled; we used the playground instead.

Young teachers reacted to this blackboard jungle by joining the Socialist Workers' Party. Our school was noted for its militancy, and we went on unofficial strike whenever we could.

At lunchtime almost the entire staff dispersed to local pubs and drank away their sorrows. When they returned slightly tipsy they could face the afternoon. One probationer returned so drunk he fell asleep on the classroom floor with all the kids dancing round him.

Sarah

Teaching at Leyton was not all gloom. When student teacher Sarah introduced herself I thought she'd do well. She'd been a pupil herself at a similar school, and knew what to expect.

'I love teaching teenage boys,' she said. 'I asked my tutor to place me in a boys' school.' German was her main subject, so she took over some of my classes. On the first day she was 20 minutes late. 'I live one hour's train journey away. I must time myself.' The next day she was 15 minutes late. 'There was a hold up.' When she was late on the third day I explained: 'As a teacher you must be on time. Classroom discipline depends on this.' She agreed: 'Sorry, it won't happen again.' The next day her excuse for lateness was extraordinary. 'I went downstairs to empty the dustbin. I slipped and the dustbin fell downstairs. I raced after it and stepped into a bucket of water. I was all wet and by the time I had changed clothes I had missed the train.'

The following week her boyfriend phoned: 'Sarah had to rush to the doctor. She'll be in later.' When she arrived she explained: 'I lost a condom inside me. The doctor had to pull it out.'

A few days later she related: 'The train caught fire. I had to catch the next one.'

'Are you quite sure?'

'You don't believe me? You can phone the station.'

Her college tutor was very satisfied with her teaching and she received her Certificate of Education. To my consternation she applied for a job at our school. I explained to the Head that her lateness didn't matter when her job was taking my lesson because I could step in, but when she had her own class there would be no one to take over. However, as she was the only applicant, the Head took her on.

Now Sarah was in her element. She decided to control the

boys by sex appeal; she wore see-through blouses which produced a miraculous effect on the 15-year-old boys. They were so eager to come to her German class that at change of lessons they would rush through the corridors banging into teachers and pupils to get to her lesson on time. Meanwhile she had the greatest difficulty in getting rid of her previous class. Boys from other classes would stop in front of her room and peep inside. At times there was such a congregation of boys outside I had to chase them away. Boys excused themselves to go to the toilet but stood outside her classroom looking through the window. Sarah was aware of all this, revelling in the attention. One day she arrived in a mini-skirt. While she walked through the classroom helping boys with their translation she bent over one boy's exercise book and saw the boy behind flashing a mirror up her skirt. She told him to stay behind after the lesson. Then she said: 'I'm going to tell my boyfriend about you. He'll come and beat you up.' The boy was terrified. Sarah enjoyed all this and told us about these scenes in the staff room.

The school had a squash court and during lunchtime some of the staff would play there. When Sarah played, instead of changing in the changing room, she would walk in her mini-shorts through the entire school. She explained: 'I must have a cup of tea first.' The boys rushed into the school building to watch her and the teacher on duty had the greatest difficulty in controlling them.

Hilda had been our Italian teacher for several years. She was in her forties, not bad looking, and as the only woman in the languages department she had been well liked by the boys. The arrival of Sarah changed all that. She was effectively ignored as the new young teacher became the focus of attention.

'Peter, what are you going to do about Sarah?'

'What am I supposed to do?'

'You can't let her walk about like that.'

'We have no school uniform for staff.'

'But her get-up is indecent. See-through blouses in a senior boys' school?'

'Hilda, that's the fashion today.'

'But they're making fun of her.'

'She doesn't seem to mind.'

'Peter, really. As a head of department I would expect you to take this more seriously.'

'I'm sorry Hilda, I do not consider it my duty to censor my colleague's dress.'

'I'm disappointed in you.'

The language advisor of Waltham Forest was so impressed by the enthusiasm Sarah aroused among the boys that at the end of her probationary period she received a letter of recommendation from the Chief Education Officer, telling her she was the best probationer of that year.

30   Exchange with Germany

'Aren't you lucky!' My colleagues at Leyton congratulated me when the British Council informed me that my exchange post in Germany was with a Catholic girls' school in Jülich.

'It'll be a contrast to our blackboard jungle,' John remarked.

'Yes, nothing could be worse than this school,' I replied.

It was 1978 and I was going to spend four months as an exchange teacher at the St Josef Schule in Jülich teaching English. Forty years ago I was in a Nazi grammar school; now I would find out what they were like today.

I attended a British Council briefing meeting. The Council official explained: 'The German education system is desperate to get away from the Nazi leadership principle. They are very democratic now, and pupils and parents are encouraged to complain about anything that's going on in the classroom. They'll complain if you give them bad marks in tests. Don't forget, in German schools test marks are most important because without a satisfactory performance pupils can't go on to the next year. Pupils' rights are safeguarded by law. It's essential to study the legal position.'

* * *

In the middle of a lesson with Class 9 at St Josef Schule, the loudspeaker blared: 'Herr Prager is wanted on the telephone.' I rushed to the office.

A voice said: 'I am the parent representative of Class 8. A father has contacted me about the test you returned yesterday. In dictation you used six words which the children had not learnt beforehand. Is this true?'

'Indeed it is. Is anything wrong?'

'According to the regulations you are not allowed to give spelling tests on words which haven't been learnt beforehand.'

'I wanted to test the pupils' ability to apply English spelling rules,' I explained.

'I see your point,' the parent representative replied, 'but it is against the law. The parent expects you to alter the girl's mark.'

The Head of the English Department confirmed that such regulations existed.

'But what use are dictations if you can't test pupils on whether they are able to apply the rules?'

'None,' replied the teacher. 'That's why we never give dictation tests.'

* * *

The following week two girls stood in front of the staff room with a note from their parents. It said.

Sehr geehrter Herr Prager,
We note that you didn't give the required 48 hours' notice for today's test. Further, you didn't state what the contents of the test will be, therefore our daughters could not revise properly. As this is against regulations we demand you postpone the test.

Again the Head of the English Department confirmed that the parents had quoted the regulations correctly.

* * *

One day I asked a pupil to read an English passage aloud to the class, to practise pronunciation. The class spokesgirl (elected according to regulations) got up: 'Herr Prager, we consider reading passages in front of the class a boring exercise. Could you do something else?'

* * *

Every time I returned a test, a queue formed with girls demanding explanations: 'Why did you mark this wrong?' 'Last year our teacher did not correct this word.' According to the regulations pupils were entitled to question their teachers and they had to answer these requests in a constructive way.

I complained to a colleague: 'I spend an entire lesson answering complaints. When am I supposed to teach?'

'Ah, you don't understand our ways yet. I always tell my pupils to see me during breaktime. This reduces the number of complaints considerably.'

Another colleague gave me a second tip: 'Remember, when you give a test, a majority of pupils must obtain at least a pass mark, otherwise, according to our laws, the test must be repeated. So don't make the test too hard.'

Remembering the Suffering

My stay in Jülich coincided with the fortieth anniversary of the pogrom on 10 November 1938. This day was to be one of the most moving of my life. It started with the early radio news bulletin giving an eyewitness account of that night of 40 years ago. Then followed a proclamation by the Federal President asking the German people never to forget these terrible times. Over half the news bulletin was taken up by this.

The schoolday started with an announcement by the head teacher: 'I want all teachers of German and history to include a lesson on the persecution of Jews.'

I asked: 'I teach English but as I was a witness to the events, may I give a personal account?' Permission was readily given and my pupils were visibly moved.

At the end of the lesson I was asked: 'How could you come back to Germany after such terrible events?'

'I can hardly blame you for the misdeeds of the older generation. Anyway, the Germany of today is completely different and deserves the support of all who believe in democracy.'

The evening television showed a torchlight parade commemorating the burning of the synagogues. During a parliamentary debate the Chancellor spoke of the collective responsibility of the German people for these crimes. He was supported by all political parties. Newspaper headlines recounted the events with photographs of burning synagogues.

On several occasions during the day I was near to tears. I had never before gone through such a heart-rending situation. An entire nation was repenting for what they had done to me and my family.

31   Israel

'Wouldn't it be nice if there was a Jewish state?'
  'But I'm not religious.'
  'Doesn't matter. Herzl wasn't religious either.'
  'This is news to me.'
  'Well he wasn't. Read his book. Most Jews who go to Palestine aren't religious.'
  We discussed this in the playground during breaktime at the Goldschmidtschule. It was 1936 and the Nazis had just made us second class citizens under the Nürnberg Laws. We dreamt of a Jewish state. But my brother Hans had been living in London for several years and my thoughts were directed towards immigration to England.
  Forty-six years later, in 1982, I became a part-time tutor at the Leo Baeck College where I taught methodology to Jewish religion teachers. I learnt about Judaism and also about Israel. At Christmas we went on a study tour to Jerusalem, and this proved to be a landmark in my life.
  Though a secular Jew, I was deeply moved as I stood with my wife at the West Wall when the Sabbath was ushered in by thousands of individual prayers. Everywhere we touched Jewish history: the walls of Jericho, Masada, Hebron.
  I read the words of the founder of the Jewish State, Ben-Gurion. He said: 'Israel must be filled with the unique content of Jewish and universal moral values. Israel must become "a light unto the nations". This just and moral society is the very condition for Israel's survival.'
  At the Damascus Gate I bought the English language edition of the Arab weekly *Al-Fahr*. There were blank spaces due to Israeli censorship. In the daily press I read reports of Israeli soldiers being found guilty of torturing Palestinians in the occupied territories. The *Jerusalem Post* stated: 'The many torture cases seem to indicate that there is a conspiracy in the

Israeli Defence Forces to maltreat captured Palestinians.'

We were taken on a tour of the occupied territories. We stopped at Hebron, where the government had confiscated land from the Palestinians and built a settlement. I walked into a Palestinian shop selling carpets. I could detect the hatred in the eyes of the shopkeeper as he watched us viewing the wares. Heinrich Heine's words came to mind (I just substituted Israel for Germany):

Denk ich an Deutschland in der Nacht
Dann bin ich um den Schlaf gebracht.

When I wake up at night and think of Germany
Sleep flies from me.

We visited the Beth Hatefutsoth museum in Tel Aviv and attended a study seminar on Jewish identity. I said to the lecturer: 'I don't like what I saw in the occupied territories. Israel is doing the wrong thing.'

'What are you doing about it?' she asked me.

Doing Something

Back in Ilford I made enquiries which led me to Mapam (now called Meretz). Their political programme said: 'There must be a partnership between Palestinians and Israelis. Israel must return the West Bank and the Gaza Strip and allow the Palestinians their own state. If Jews have their own state, why not the Palestinians? The military occupation of Arab territories has a corrupting influence on Israeli society.' I joined and was elected to the Mazkirut. I decided to give talks in synagogues and other Jewish organizations on peace and reconciliation with Palestinians. I was always accompanied by an Arab.

During Netanyahu's premiership my task was difficult. I received few invitations and my reception was not always friendly. On one occasion a letter said: 'Please do not bring an Arab for security reasons.'

The Lebanese flautist Wissam Boustany had accompanied me on many visits. When an audience became hostile he took

176

out his flute and played a melody on peace. It always calmed them. Ibrahim, a Palestinian from Hebron has also joined me. At Sinclair House he told the audience: 'I was driven from my home by Israeli soldiers and I hated all Jews. When I studied at the LSE in London I played in a basketball team, and suddenly realized that my team mates were Jews. How could I hate these people? Slowly I realized that hate solves nothing and now I campaign for a two-state solution.' His 18-year-old daughter accompanied him and also supported his plea for tolerance. The audience was so impressed we were asked to repeat our talks at the B'nai B'rith Golda Meir Lodge.

When asked to talk to the Ben Gurion Lodge in Southgate my reception was very different. The secretary wrote: 'I understand you will be bringing an Arab friend with you. There are some fervent Zionists in our Lodge. I hope he will not provoke them into heated arguments. Our atmosphere is usually very friendly and we would like it to remain so.' I answered: 'No doubt you are aware that Mapam was among the early pioneers. We are Zionists who have fought for a two-state solution since the formation of our State.' I approached the day with apprehension. I was to meet Ramsey Amin, an Egyptian, at the entrance. To my surprise two Arabs were there.

'Hello Peter,' Ramsey greeted me. 'Meet Abbas Shiblak, a friend of mine from Ramalla. He is Head of Information of the Arab League. He will be much better for answering questions. I hope you don't mind.' My heart sank but I said: 'That's fine. Hello Abbas.'

He turned out to be very conciliatory. I was the one who spoiled the atmosphere. A Likudnik kept on interrupting: 'Why has Arafat still not abrogated the Palestinian Charter which calls for the destruction of the State of Israel?'

I answered: 'On 22 April 1996 the PLO cancelled those parts of the Charter which called for the destruction of Israel.'

'No, he never did.'

I continued: 'This cancellation was accepted by the Labour Government of Israel, by the United States, by Europe and by the whole world.'

'Nonsense!'

'Netanyahu refused to accept it.'

'Quite right.'

Now I became hot under the collar. 'Netanyahu has taken note of a certain person, whose name I won't mention, who said that if you repeat a lie often enough people will believe you.'

'What do you mean?'

Turning to the Likudnik I continued: 'Obviously you have been taken in by these lies.'

'Rubbish! Stop him!'

A member of the audience got up and advanced towards the chair: 'Why was this man invited?'

Amidst uproar the chairman shouted. 'Please calm yourselves. Breaktime. Refreshments are now served.'

With tea and cakes things became more friendly. Several members agreed with my ideas.

One member, a rabbi, asked to be put on the Meretz mailing list. 'You know, my daughter is one of yours,' he remarked.

During a demonstration in front of No. 10 Downing Street organized by the Palestine Solidarity Committee, a BBC reporter asked me: 'Why do you demonstrate with Palestinians?'

I answered: 'Because I am a Jew. I feel it is essential for Jews to show that Palestinians have the same rights to a homeland as we have.'

The breakdown of the peace talks under Barak have saddened me. Recently my wife and I spent a holiday in Rome. As we walked through the centre of the city, the uniform of the police suddenly changed. We were in the Vatican. It shows how Jerusalem could exist in a united city, with two sovereign governments and two separate police forces. I hope Israel will realize this and that peace can still be achieved.

32   What's Wrong with Me?

In 1939 Mr Flateau, my guarantor, said to Hans, my brother: 'I'm sorry to say that Peter lacks a sense of humour.' This was viewed as a serious shortcoming and Mr Flateau was sure that there was something wrong with me.

At weekends we went regularly to the Flateau's caravan in Roydon, Hertfordshire, and on Saturday nights we visited the local pub. The jokes, the banter and the idle talk were strange to me.

'Come on Peter, join in!'

'Alright,' I said but stayed in my corner sipping orange juice.

Everybody was chatting and laughing, and I felt like an outsider ready to cry at any moment. The Flateaus expected me to join in the fun. After all, they said, I wasn't in Germany any more. They were good, kind people but they complained bitterly to Hans that I didn't seem to appreciate what they had done for me. On the other hand, I considered their attitude frivolous and unfeeling.

In any case how could I change myself? Was there something wrong with me?

When the Nazis were in power, family gatherings were sombre affairs.

'Did you hear, Onkel Richard got his affidavit for America?'

'What's his quota number?'

'He's got to wait till 1942.'

'Good God.'

'Onkel Paul says he won't get a visa for Brazil unless he's got 10,000 Marks. As he has to pay a 90 per cent emigration tax he's not got enough money.'

'Onkel Georg says he can get a visa for Schanghai without any difficulty.'

'What's he going to do there?'

'Become a coolie.'

Such discussions were carried on in hushed voices, all the doors in the flat were closed and a cushion was placed over the phone. My experience at the Grunewald Gymnasium did nothing to lighten the gloom which pervaded our entire life. I felt I was living in a huge trap, the walls of which were slowly but surely closing in on me. A few weeks after the November pogrom, the first concentration camp victims were released. At that time extermination was not yet Nazi policy. Their aim was to terrorize us. When Vati was released from Sachsenhausen he told me that he had to sign a statement swearing that he would tell nothing of what he had seen or experienced in the camp on pain of re-arrest. He asked me not to make it difficult for him, and not to ask. But his looks told everything.

But there were also cultural differences which made integration into English society difficult. In comparison with English people, Germans are rather formal when meeting strangers, partly due to the fact that the German language is less democratic than English. In English we call everybody 'you', but in German one distinguishes between strangers, who are addressed as 'Sie', and family and close friends who are addressed 'du'. In English the nearest equivalent is first names, which often happens at a first meeting.

In the circles in which the Flateaus moved, everyone called everyone else by their first name.

'Peter, meet my friend John. Peter is a refugee from Germany.'

I was supposed to call a complete stranger by his first name; I just couldn't do it. I replied, 'Hello, Mr Smith.'

I was even too diffident to call Mr and Mrs Flateau 'Mary' and 'Sydney' as they expected me to. The Flateaus didn't understand my hesitation and thought I was purposely trying to distance myself. What was wrong with me?

* * *

In 1950 I was teaching Geography at St. Chad's Secondary School, Tilbury. I showed a film on Israel. A class of sullen-looking children who had just been liberated from the camps were having an art lesson. They were drawing pictures of people surrounded by barbed wire. A few weeks later the same children drew pictures of gardens with flowers. A little girl showed her drawing to the teacher and was smiling. The commentator said: 'This is the first smile in the class. The teacher is winning. Soon all children will laugh. The battle for rehabilitation will be won.'

I watched the film with fascination. Suddenly the scales fell from my eyes. Those children were me! My five years in Nazi Germany were like a concentration camp. I came to this country and couldn't smile because the Nazi environment had traumatized me. I did not really lack a sense of humour. There was nothing wrong with me.

33   Repentance

I thought the Old Boys' Association of the Grunewald Gymnasium (now called Walther Rathenau Schule) would be interested to read about what happened to me at their school. So I sent them extracts for their journal *Die Alte Schule*.

A few weeks later a letter arrived from Fritz Schulze in Bielefeld: 'I was in your class and read your article. Do you remember me? Your account has devastated me. I can't recall the song with the refrain 'When Jewish blood gushes forth from your knife...' I never realized how you felt. During the war I was in the air force but was not engaged in bombing England. I am a doctor and a member of the campaign, Doctors against Nuclear War. I must speak to you to discuss things. I want to visit you for a weekend.'

I agreed to collect Fritz from Heathrow. I said I'd carry a copy of *The Times* so that he would recognize me.

Fritz arrived. He was slim, my height, and though the same age he looked younger. We went for walks and I took him to the theatre. 'You must come to our yearly reunion,' he said. I was waiting for him to 'discuss things', but he didn't; he wanted to find out how I would treat him, and he seemed satisfied.

At the re-union Sylvia and I stayed in a motel near the Wannsee. The welcoming dinner was at seven o'clock. As we entered the dining room there was applause. Fritz commented: 'We've met for many years but only with your presence are we a proper reunion.'

We visited the Grunewald Gymnasium where the Head showed us round. In the hall was a display of old documents.

'Look, here is Peter Prager's name!' exclaimed Günther Löwe. It showed my file from April 1933. Next to my name, very clearly written was 'Jew'.

* * *

During the two days of our gathering the 'old boys' were eager to tell me their stories.

Günther Löwe

I was taken prisoner by the Americans in North Africa. We received American newspapers and were interested in the daily army communiqués. Allied and German communiqués were side by side. The German reports differed sharply from the Allied and we took it for granted that they had been doctored. More prisoners arrived and they brought the latest German newspapers with the German army communiqués. We compared. They were identical with the German communiqué printed by the Americans. So the Americans printed the truth – something our side never did. Slowly I understood how a free press works. It was my first lesson in democracy.

Jürgen Krause

Before I went to the Russian front my mother gave me a Bible which I carried with me throughout the war. 'You're doing God's work,' my mother said. I was taken prisoner by the Russians at Kursk. We had been told that the Russians took no prisoners, so were waiting for death. Instead I was sent a thousand kilometres east to join a German prisoner-of-war camp. My first question: 'How long have you been here?' The reply came: 'Six months.' This was the first indication to me that our government told lies.

Werner Scherkel

I had my army training in Weimar. Our barracks were next to the SS. I envied the SS because they only had a short distance to their camp in Buchenwald while we had a one-hour march to our training camp. We had been told that hardened prisoners were sent to the concentration camp. Only after the war we learnt that these camps were outside the jurisdiction of the courts. We guessed that conditions were harsh but we knew nothing of the torture and killings.

Erna Brunner (wife)

When Zeitz was liberated by the Americans they put huge posters on noticeboards with photos of Buchenwald. We stood round these pictures with disgust. 'That's typical American war propaganda. They're trying to make us hate our government. Of course they probably made mistakes but they would never have done things like this. These photos are faked.' Slowly the truth sank in. It took us a long time to get over the shock.

Hans Röstler

When I saw the first Jew walking along the Kurfürstendamm with the Star of David I sat on a bench and cried. What was I supposed to do?

Ulrich Hübner

When I learned the truth about the Hitler regime I had sleepless nights. I always believed in God. Now every stone in Germany reminded me of my shame, and I knew I could not remain in the country. I went to Canada, but my memory went with me and I had no rest. So I returned to Germany and then I decided to visit Israel. I took my Bible and tried to recognize the places mentioned in the Old Testament. I was amazed by the friendliness shown by the Israelis. Every year now I go to the Holy Land on a pilgrimage. I have to tell you this: I'm sure you're right that this song was sung in the class – but I was not present, you must believe me.

Klaus Schnabel

A Polish unit of volunteers was attached to our regiment. They received horrifying reports about the treatment of their people back home. Our commanding officer wrote to the general of our division: 'Could you please investigate what is going on in Poland? The morale of our Polish volunteers is poor as a result of these reports.' A few days later an answer came from Goebbels: 'Your business is to fight for the Fatherland. Don't concern yourself with matters which are none of your business.' I was thinking what kind of a war are we fighting? It was too late when I woke up to the truth. What was I supposed to do?

Guntram Mullert

I've just written an autobiography. I called it *How I Grew Up to become the Companion of the Devil.*

Fritz Deutsch

I was shattered when I read your account of our school. I am ashamed. Yes, that's how it was. I can remember every episode which you recount. I've written a book about this period and Berlin TV want to make a film. Would you be prepared to come to Berlin and be interviewed?

(Fritz wrote this in a letter to me, and I agreed to be interviewed.)

* * *

The song with the refrain 'When Jewish blood gushes forth from your knife ...' caused quite a stir. An old boy from another class challenged me: 'We know this song existed. But it was never sung in our school. You will not find anybody to verify your story.' I was beginning to doubt my memory. After all, I was only ten years old at the time. Perhaps I had heard the song on the radio and only imagined it was sung in the school.

Two years later the following letter from New York appeared in the school magazine: 'I've just heard of your journal. I must tell you of an event which has been on my mind all these years. In 1933 I was in the *Oberprima*. I was 19 years of age. One day our music teacher appeared in SS uniform and said he wanted us to sing a new song. It had the refrain 'When Jewish blood gushes forth from your knife ...' The entire class stood up in protest and walked out. I shall never forget this. It kept my faith in decency.

* * *

Why have I been going to these reunions regularly? In 1933 I felt left out. I thought, 'What a shame I'm not an Aryan. I can't join in with the others.' If I had not been a Jew I have no doubt that I would have been carried away by the enthusiasm created by the Nazis just like my schoolmates. I would have fought for a false idea and finally become terribly disillusioned like the others. At last year's reunion my wife asked, 'When you heard of the resettlement of Jews in Poland did you ever think what might happen to them?'

Jürgen Krause answered for all, 'We pushed it aside. You must understand that we were under the spell of the greatest and cleverist propagandist the world has ever seen; exposed to him since we were ten years of age. Now we are all ashamed [*wir schämen uns*].'

His remarks met with everyone's approval.

When people repent you must offer your hand in reconciliation.

I did.